IT'S THE S
NOT THE COLLEGE

THE EXPERIMENT

BECAUSE EVERY BOOK IS A TEST OF NEW IDEAS

IT'S THE

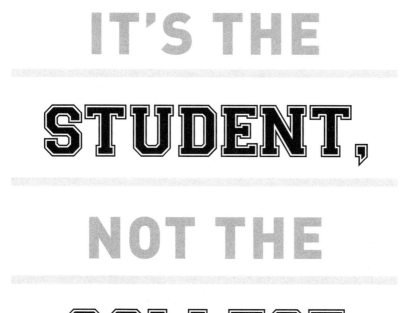

STUDENT,

NOT THE

COLLEGE

THE SECRETS OF SUCCEEDING
AT ANY SCHOOL—WITHOUT GOING
BROKE OR CRAZY

KRISTIN M. WHITE

THE EXPERIMENT
NEW YORK

IT'S THE STUDENT, NOT THE COLLEGE: *The Secrets of Succeeding at Any School—Without Going Broke or Crazy*

The Experiment, LLC
220 East 23rd Street, Suite 301
New York, NY 10010-4674
www.theexperimentpublishing.com

The Experiment's books are available at special discounts when purchased in bulk for premiums and sales promotions as well as for fund-raising or educational use. For details, contact us at info@theexperimentpublishing.com.

Library of Congress Cataloging-in-Publication Data

White, Kristin M.
  It's the student, not the college : the secrets of succeeding at any schoolwithout going broke or crazy / Kristin M. White.
     pages cm
  Includes bibliographical references and index.
  ISBN 978-1-61519-237-3 (pbk.) — ISBN 978-1-61519-238-0 (ebook)
1. Universities and colleges—Admission. 2. Universities and colleges—Entrance requirements. 3. College choice. 4. College cost. I. Title.
  LB2351.W48 2015
  378.1'61—dc23
                              2014044242
ISBN 978-1-61519-237-3
Ebook ISBN 978-1-61519-238-0

Cover design by Jason Alejandro
Author photograph by Megan Dey Photography
Text design by Pauline Neuwirth, Neuwirth & Associates, Inc.

Manufactured in the United States of America
Distributed by Workman Publishing Company, Inc.
Distributed simultaneously in Canada by Thomas Allen & Son Ltd.

First printing March 2015
10 9 8 7 6 5 4 3 2 1

Contents

PART THREE
WHAT YOU *SHOULD* CONSIDER WHEN CHOOSING A SCHOOL

Introduction

America has college fever. There has been no other time in history when so many people from so many diverse groups have been so focused on college: how to select a school, how to pay for it, and how it will affect a young life. And it's not just any college that we are focused on. Parents today want their child to go to a "good" college, preferably one that is selective and highly ranked, and many students expect no less for themselves.

Parents, myself included, have been led to believe that it is our responsibility, even our calling, to do everything we can to position our children so they will have good options for college and in life. We hear constantly from the media, high schools, colleges, and other parents about the importance of attending a "good college." We are told that top colleges are where all the connections are made, skills are learned, and prestigious companies come to recruit. Top colleges have the best professors, facilities, and educational quality; and we parents should push to get the best for our children.

We worry, often in silence, over secret fears: If my student doesn't attend a "good college," will he be a failure? Will he be one of those young adults who moves home after college and works at a string of hourly-wage jobs as he struggles to start a career? Will he be less likely to get into a graduate school or to succeed there? Will he have trouble making transitions in the middle of his career because of his "no-name college"? Will he be forever a step behind his peers who went to top colleges, or worse, could he be doomed to a lifetime of career unhappiness because of his weak college background?

Many teenagers have similar worries. Some are fixated on getting into their "dream school," while others worry that they haven't found the perfect college yet. They have their own secret fears: What if I bomb the SAT and can't get in anywhere? What if I disappoint my parents? Why am I devoting so much of my life to getting into a top college when the admission rates are so low that it may never happen anyway? Will I end up with fewer career options if I don't go to a good college?

These fears and concerns have led to a new expectation that teenagers will run a gauntlet of "meaningful" extracurricular activities, expensive tutors, and SAT-prep courses, which often incur greater expenses than their families can afford. Parents hope for a launching pad that will give their young-adult children a fighting chance in today's competitive job market, and the kids hope for it, too. That launching pad is a top college, and we will do anything it takes to help our children get there.

Indeed, there is a mystique about elite colleges, which I'll address at length in Chapter 1. But the surprising news is that the premise behind the top-college admissions mania is false. Attending an elite college has very little impact on a student's career success, future earnings, or well-being.

Let that sink in. If it sounds counterintuitive, I don't blame you. Many graduates of top colleges have gone on to fame and fortune: John D. Rockefeller, Jr. (Brown), President Barack Obama (Columbia), United States Supreme Court justice Ruth Bader Ginsburg (Cornell), Theodor "Dr. Seuss" Geisel (Dartmouth), comedian Conan O'Brien (Harvard), Amazon founder Jeff Bezos (Princeton), LinkedIn CEO Jeffrey Weiner (Penn), Hewlett Packard CEO Meg Whitman

(Princeton) . . . the list could go for pages, and that's just the Ivy League!

What I hope to convince you is that we have made a mistake by attributing Ivy League graduates' success to their colleges. In fact, elite universities do not make their students succeed; rather, they identify (and admit) applicants who will go on to be successful. In other words, the students who are accepted to Ivies already have what it takes to achieve great things. A student's motivation, academic profile, and ambition are really what matter; the name on his diploma means very little. You don't have to take my word for it: data backs me up, and I will discuss it in detail in Chapter 2.

If the college attended doesn't determine success, what is a student to do? Relax and watch television all day, since there's no point in trying to get into a selective college? No! Certain young people excel whether or not they go to elite colleges, and they don't do it by sitting back and hoping to luck out. They take specific steps in high school and college to ensure their future success. Any student—whether still in high school, about to start college, or midway through her college experience—can examine what it is that makes these elite students do so well and adopt some of their practices for herself.

Part Two will explore those practices and lay out a plan that students can personalize to develop what I call the "Success Profile"—the mindset, focus, study habits, achievements, grit, and personal relationships that lead to academic, leadership, employment, and personal fulfillment in the future. Incidentally, many of the traits and habits in the Success Profile are also in demand among college admissions officers—but I hope you will think of your efforts as an investment in yourself, not just as a way to impress the committee at a specific school. Remember: admissions officers select students who are already poised to do great things, regardless of their college choice.

Finally, Part Three will provide guidance on what *is* important in making a college decision, once you've gotten past all of the hype surrounding college selectivity. It examines the vital importance of finding a "financial fit" (page 156) for your family and offers some predictions about where college admissions and finances might be headed in the future.

Most chapters include personal stories from students with whom I have worked and sidebars about specific opportunities to develop a Success Profile.

I hope you'll find it reassuring to know that a student can develop himself to improve his future prospects, and that his likelihood of success isn't correlated to "beating the odds" and getting into an elite college. This book explains exactly how students can prepare themselves for future success— and why following this plan is better than focusing on "getting in."

Note: I will use masculine and feminine pronouns alternately throughout this book. The choice of pronoun is not intended to imply gender-specific differences in the information or advice.

PART ONE

THE TRUTH

ABOUT COLLEGE,

SELECTIVITY,

AND SUCCESS

Busting the Elite-College Mystique

The college admissions culture of today—the expensive, stress-inducing quest for a top-college acceptance letter—is far over-hyped. Highly rated colleges have tremendous importance in popular culture and in the minds and hearts of families. Attending one holds special cachet. Many of us continue to believe that top colleges offer a golden ticket to success, or at least an easier path to a good career.

This elite-college mystique is continually propped up by the media, which loves the college admissions drama: the *Wall Street Journal* and *The New York Times* each average ten articles a month on the topic during the school year. Major motion pictures feature plot lines about the college process, including *Admission, How I Got Into College*, and blockbusters like *Risky Business* and *Legally Blonde*. If that isn't enough to keep your mind on college admissions, characters in hit television shows such as *Gilmore Girls, Friday Night Lights, The Sopranos*, and *Modern Family* have also modeled the hope and anxiety of applying to college.

In some communities, college decals adorn the back windshields of cars. Parents discuss college admissions at cocktail parties, on the sidelines of sporting events, or anywhere else that they get together. There is great status in having a child attend a top college, and sometimes there is embarrassment when a son or daughter enrolls at a college that is not impressive to others in the community.

These parents—and there are many of them—have bought into the mystique. We have put select colleges on a pedestal and come to believe that they are more special than they really are. Our assumption that certain colleges are the best continues to spawn new misguided beliefs: that "everyone else" manages to pay for their children's tuition, so we can too; that it's impossible to make valuable career connections at a state school; that the intelligence of professors and students at elite schools will raise our children's academic performance by osmosis; and so on. Yet, if you consider the facts, all of this turns out to be false.

In this book's introduction, I proposed that elite colleges do no better than other colleges at ensuring happiness and financial well-being; Chapter 2 will dig deeper into the research that supports this. But to look at college this way, to really call out the top colleges as no better than many other options, requires a cultural paradigm shift. To understand why this shift in the way that we think about the college experience is needed, we first need to know where we are, and how we got here.

STORIES OF THE MYTH IN ACTION

At the KIPP Academy charter school in Tulsa, Oklahoma, low-income middle school students who aspire to be the first in their families to attend college know all about Harvard, Yale, and Princeton. Rather than a room number, each classroom is given the name of a top college. The school is also decorated with banners from selective colleges, which the students see as they move from their math class in the

Amherst room to science in the Stanford room. The teachers at KIPP promote excellence, and admission to an Ivy League–type college is considered an ideal that every KIPP student has the potential to reach. KIPP runs eighty middle schools throughout the United States, so its message of educational opportunity is reaching students from San Jose to New York City—as is its assertion that attending an Ivy League school is the apotheosis of that opportunity.

In Phoenix, Arizona, more than two hundred people pack a hotel conference room to listen to a college presentation given by the admissions offices of Harvard, Georgetown, Duke, Stanford, and the University of Pennsylvania. These five colleges are travel partners, and together they journey throughout the world, introducing the idea of selective colleges to families who may not have considered them. They are turning over every rock, looking for accomplished and interesting young people and encouraging them to apply to their colleges. Families in Phoenix listen with hope to the descriptions of these world-class institutions and are often surprised to hear that, with financial aid, the cost to attend may be within their reach.

In Shanghai, China, fourteen-year-old Zhang Min spends nine hours a day in a specialized "training school" designed to teach her English and prepare her for the Secondary School Admission Test (SSAT), a standardized test required for admission to American boarding schools. Like many others of Shanghai's elite, Zhang Min has taken a year off from high school to attend this program, with the hopes of gaining a coveted spot at a rigorous American boarding school. She and her family believe that this is the first and most important step toward admission to a prestigious American university (which, in turn, is considered the essential springboard to an illustrious career).

In Short Hills, New Jersey, seventeen-year-old Matthew is up at one am studying for the ACT. He has already taken the

SAT twice and is now trying the ACT at the suggestion of his tutor. Matthew meets with three tutors each week who help him with his staggering academic load of five AP classes, which he tries to balance with soccer and band practices. When Matthew gets tired, he thinks about his dream of attending Stanford. He envisions himself at his first-choice school and is able to continue studying. Matthew is overloaded with academic work and test preparation activities, most of which he has undertaken only to help him get into his dream school.

The recent explosion of interest in selective colleges has made these stories all too common. Names like Harvard and Princeton have become synonymous with ambition, success, and excellence. They are aspirational words used to motivate students. No longer are these colleges' images tied to the white Christian male establishment that dominated their student bodies for hundreds of years. Families today believe that top colleges are open and welcoming, looking for talented, hardworking young people, and paying no regard to a student's finances or personal background. And parents and students alike believe that it's worth doing almost anything to get in.

THE NEW AMERICAN DREAM

College represents more than just four years of coursework in an area of academic interest. We believe that a top college degree will propel a student to new heights, set in motion rags-to-riches stories, and open any possible door. Americans look to Barack Obama and Bill Clinton, two men who attended selective colleges—Columbia and Georgetown, respectively—and whose college experiences took them away from their hometowns and humble beginnings and set them on the path to the White House.

With such heady expectations, it's understandable that, for many families, the college decision letter brings great joy or anguish. In 2012, the Target corporation got into the mix with a commercial showing actual video of teens getting the good news about a college acceptance. The heartwarming ad (which featured big smiles, shrieks of delight, and lines such as "I'm going to college; it's official!") ran during the Olympics and was widely tweeted about, since it captured this rite of passage so well. Thousands of students have posted their own college acceptance videos on YouTube, and most of them consider their acceptance the greatest achievement of their young lives. The acceptance letter is the ultimate trophy, the stamp of approval that says your past has been exceptional and your future will be outstanding.

College admissions is now thoroughly a part of the American Dream, but it wasn't always that way. When universities were given the mandate to create diverse incoming classes, they began to recruit and promote themselves to students across the country and all over the world. At the same time, there was a massive increase in financial aid availability in the form of education loans. As a result, domestic and international families who previously would have been content with local universities were now considering elite colleges that they hoped would give their children a brighter future. Students began to apply in droves.

In 1991, 8,800 students applied to Princeton, and 19,000 applied to Cornell. Fast-forward to 2014, when 26,600 students applied for essentially the same number of spots at Princeton, and 43,000 hoped to be accepted to Cornell. It is true that the population of eighteen-year-olds went up slightly during that time, but the driving force behind the increase in applications was a cultural shift. Elite private colleges attained a new and prized status in the eyes of people who would never have considered them before.

Of course it is true that education fits right in with the

American Dream, with its goals of moving up in the world, doing better than one's parents, and becoming financially secure. Young Americans have always been told that if they study hard, they can be anything they want to be in life. It is this belief that has brought many immigrants to the United States in search of better lives for their children. And, certainly, the evidence overwhelmingly supports the importance of a college education for future earnings and other positive outcomes. But when did we get the idea that studying hard and attending the local state university were not enough?

Some people believe that if a college degree is a step on the path to the American Dream, then surely a selective college degree will get you there faster. Every family is supposed to want what is "best" for their child, and many of us have come to view attending an elite college as the best option for all children. After all, if so many leaders throughout history have graduated from Ivy League colleges, these colleges must be the key to becoming a leader. Yet, as I have suggested, this belief is the result of a fundamental misconception: that the Ivy League *makes*, rather than *collects*, successful people. Elite colleges select the best, most promising students, who are already succeeding and capable of even more. And even that idea of selectivity, which is a huge contributor to the mystique around college admissions, has not always been true.

A SHORT AND SURPRISING HISTORY OF IVY LEAGUE ADMISSIONS

Can you imagine Harvard placing an advertisement in *The New York Times* asking students to apply? Would you be further surprised to see the ad mention that 185 out of 210 applicants were accepted in the past year (an 88 percent acceptance rate)? Or to see that entrance exams were given

YALE LAW SCHOOL,
NEW-HAVEN, CONN.
THEODORE D. WOOLSEY, D.D., LL.D., President.
HENRY DUTTON, LL.D., Professor.
Course two years. No preliminary examination.
Students can enter or leave at any time.
The first term commences the eigth Monday after the last Thursday but one of July.
The second term commences the first Monday before the first Wednesuay of May.
Fall vacation, eight weeks. Spring vacation, three weeks.
Recess of two weeks, embracing Christmas and New Year.
Tuition first year, $80; second year, $70; less than a year, $10 per month.
Tuition payable in advance, or to be secured, except for satisfactory reasons.

Harvard was far from alone in its low standards.

continuously up until the week before classes started? In 1870, advertising was crucial for universities to reach the limited number of young male citizens who had the funds and educational background to pursue a college degree.[1]

A century earlier, college freshmen were often the age of today's middle-school students. In that era, children who were wealthy enough to receive an education were usually tutored at home. When they knew enough Latin, Greek, and mathematics to pass the university entrance exam, they enrolled, whether they were twelve, fourteen, or eighteen years old. For example, John Adams enrolled at Harvard in 1751 at age sixteen, and Thomas Jefferson was also sixteen when he joined the freshman class at the College of William & Mary in 1760. It's hard to believe that the elite universities of today were once relatively nonselective programs for young teens.

It wasn't until the early twentieth century that the top colleges had anything similar to the admissions process that we have today. In 1905, Harvard ended its own exam administration and used tests from the College Entrance Examination Board, which tripled the number of testing locations.[2] Most colleges dropped their Greek and Latin requirements, and this opened up the applicant pool to public-school students, who were not traditionally offered these classes. The wealthy elite who had dominated enrollment in the colleges for so long began to see outsiders passing the admissions exams in large numbers. This new diversity was not seen as a positive development. In particular, there was concern about the many Jewish students applying to Harvard, Yale, and Princeton. And thus began a discussion within the colleges about the inclusion of factors beyond the admissions exam when deciding whether to admit a student.

Radcliffe Heermance, the director of admissions at Princeton from 1922 to 1950, was called "the keeper of the Princeton gate" by *Newsweek*.[3] In 1922, there had been a record high of twenty-five Jewish students in the freshman class of 582.[4] Heermance introduced several initiatives to "shape" the class as he and others in the administration saw fit. Ironically, many of his admissions processes, which were arguably started to keep Jewish students out of the Ivy League, have persisted to this day as ways to promote a diverse campus community.

Heermance relied heavily on the personal interview, in which interviewers could assess a students' "appearance, deportment, manners, and *not least*, ethnic and religious background" (italics mine).[5] He required several personal references and asked that one be from "some Princeton graduate in the community" who could provide "a confidential statement concerning the boy's character and standing."[6] Heermance stated that boys with weaker academic backgrounds should still be admitted after looking at "the applicant's athletic and extracurricular activities and . . . a personal interview."[7] By 1930, Heermance was quite successful in his mission, with only eleven Jewish students and ninety-four public-school boys entering the freshman class.[8]

The years after World War II provided a flood of applicants to the elite colleges. President Franklin D. Roosevelt signed the Serviceman's Readjustment Act (commonly known as the GI Bill) in 1944, which provided college or trade-school tuition to returning veterans. Colleges throughout the country saw a surge in applicants, and Harvard posted a 55-percent acceptance rate in 1946, one of its lowest on record at the time.[9] However, looking at numbers available in 1950, we can tell that Harvard still had exclusionary admissions practices that benefitted traditional boarding-school students from wealthy white families. Of the forty-eight applicants from Groton, St. Paul's, and St. Mark's, forty-six were accepted.[10] Relying on the exam alone had not given the admissions committee leeway to consider the subjective aspects of a student's application, but the introduction of interviews, references, and a focus on extracurricular activities and "character" were effective measures for shaping the student body as the administration envisioned it.

In 1959, Harvard formed a Faculty Special Committee on College Admission Policy to deliberate about what qualities and factors should be considered in the admissions process.[11] They spent nearly a year collecting data on the academic performance of various groups of students, including public-school students and private-school students, athletes and non-athletes, alumni children and those with no Harvard affiliation, and scholarship students and those paying their own way.[12] One striking finding of the study was an extreme underperformance of the boarding-school students compared to the smaller number of public-school students. The study analyzed statistics from seventy-nine high schools that had placed four or more students in three Harvard classes. The researchers found that the academic performance of the boarding-school students was in the bottom half of the seventy-nine high schools, with populations from their common feeder schools St. Mark's, St. Paul's, and Middlesex ranking "63rd, 65th, and 76th, respectively." Not one of the top thirty high schools represented at Harvard was an Eastern boarding school. Ten of the top twelve schools were in New York City, and the other two were in Philadelphia. The study noted that "the New England private schools supply over 40% (187/463) of our flunk-outs and drops-outs, but less than 20% (68/344) of our magnas and summas."[13]

These revelations sparked debate at Harvard that may have contributed to the change in admission policy that came about soon afterward. The social transformation of the 1960s brought great change to Harvard, Yale, Princeton, and most other top colleges. Quickly and furiously, they began accepting women, African Americans, Asian Americans, immigrants, and larger numbers of Jewish students. In 1960, there was one African American freshman at Princeton; by 1972, black students represented 10.4 percent of the freshman class, the largest percentage in any class before or since that time.[14] Princeton had purposely transformed its admissions policies. The school undertook a strategy of recruiting visits to areas with large minority populations, and school representatives built relationships with a broad number of secondary schools in order to get a diverse group of applicants. Other colleges followed suit, and the focus on academic excellence and a diverse class became the hallmark of the admissions process.

The American college mystique is built upon the belief that selective colleges are inherently better. The history of the colleges and of their alumni is a big part of the mystique. Because Harvard has been around for so long and has so many illustrious graduates, people assume that it was always selective and always attracted true scholars. This simply isn't true: there was a time when these colleges were advertising for students and then turning away top-performing students in favor of the white New England establishment.

TODAY AND YESTERDAY: A LOOK AT A
TYPICAL IVY LEAGUE APPLICANT

The last twenty years have seen unprecedented growth in applications to selective colleges, as well as intensified pressure on their applicants. By comparing a valedictorian and Ivy League hopeful of today with the same high school's valedictorian from twenty years earlier, we can see how dramatically our view of college and admissions has changed.

In 1991, the valedictorian from a suburban high school in Summit, New Jersey, or Westport, Connecticut, was likely to get accepted to several Ivy League colleges. Kevin was one of these students, and his SAT scores matched his high grades. He dabbled in a few activities, lettered in lacrosse, and had some local leadership experience. Kevin assumed he would get accepted to several elite schools, maybe not Harvard, but certainly Cornell or Penn. He took the SAT once after reviewing several large SAT prep books. He visited a few colleges with his family during the summer before his senior year. With no clear first choice in mind that fall, Kevin decided to apply Regular Decision to seven colleges. He competed with about 20,000 other students to earn one of the 6,200 acceptances awarded by Cornell that year. Kevin enrolled at Cornell and his parents paid the $17,338 out-of-state tuition and room-and-board bill mostly with savings, but also with a small amount from private loans.[15]

About twenty-five years later, Emily is the valedictorian of the same high school that Kevin attended. She has been preparing for college for as long as she can remember, and she is committed to doing everything she can to get into a top college. As a child, she had music and art lessons and tried almost every sport, as her parents hoped she would find her passion or one activity in which to excel. By high school, she had developed a rigid schedule for herself, so that she could fit several hours of study into a day already packed with travel team practice and volunteer projects. She tried several approaches to test prep, including working with a tutor, taking an online Kaplan class, and reviewing problems on Khan Academy (see page 205). After three attempts at the SAT, she finally had a combination of scores that resulted in a "super score" that she was happy with. Emily and her parents visited more than twenty colleges, and on one trip she found her dream school. After careful consideration of facts and weighing her "gut feeling," she decided that Cornell was her first-choice college.

THE EXPLOSION OF COLLEGE ADMISSIONS INTEREST BY THE NUMBERS

SCHOOL	APPLICATIONS IN 1991	APPLICATIONS IN 2014
Princeton	8,800	26,600
Yale	13,000	30,900
Cornell	22,940	43,000
University of Connecticut	13,000	29,500

Note: Figures have been rounded.

- There were 819,000 international students at American universities in 2013[16]
- More than half of college students apply to at least four colleges, up 10 percent since 2008. Many apply to fifteen, and some apply to over twenty[17]
- Six percent of college-bound students and 26 percent of high-achieving students (with SAT scores above 1,150 on a 1,600 scale, or an ACT of 25 or above) work with an independent educational consultant[18]
- Kaplan made $293 million in test-prep revenue from 415,000 students in 2013[19]

The fall of Emily's senior year is a whirlwind, with a heavy homework load from five AP courses and weekly meetings with her tutors and educational consultant. She knows that there is an advantage to applying Early Decision, so she works on the Cornell application, as well as five other non-binding Early Action applications. Emily's application is one of 43,000 read by the Cornell admissions office. Cornell gives offers to 6,220 students, but Emily does not receive good news. Instead, she enrolls at New York University. Although NYU is an excellent university, Emily is disappointed that she was denied by her dream school and didn't measure up to the Ivy League. Plus, much of her $62,000 yearly bill for tuition and room and board will be paid with loans that she and her parents will need to pay back, most likely over the course of many years. Still, Emily sees no alternative to enrolling at the "best" school that accepted her. What would become of her otherwise?

THE BUSINESS OF COLLEGE ADMISSIONS

The keen interest in college admissions today has spawned new growth fields that have continued to expand even as the economy has slowed. Test prep has been big business for many years, with major players, such as Kaplan and the *Princeton Review*, and local tutors, who charge up to $200 an hour in some markets. Online classes and tutoring have now surpassed in-person sessions as the most popular way to prepare for the SAT or ACT.

The college-admissions frenzy is also a factor in the growth of subject tutoring and tutoring for younger students. In wealthy communities, it is not uncommon for students in the first and second grades to have weekly tutors. Many will continue with tutors all the way through high school and college. In competitive high schools, even strong students are provided with tutors in math and science to assure a high grade in coursework and on SAT subject tests.

According to Mark Sklarow of the Independent Educational Consultants Association (IECA), educational consulting has been an enormous growth field, with the number of new consultants growing an average of 20 percent annually from 2009 to 2014. Independent educational consultants (IECs), including myself, are professionals who help families with the college search and application process. More than two thousand consultants are members of the IECA, a professional association with membership requirements and an ethical code. Although there is a misconception among some families that consultants are unscrupulous or provide an unnecessary service, a good IEC has an extensive background in education and is able to focus on a small number of clients, encouraging them to consider their interests and goals and find a good fit. Most have reasonable rates, and over 90 percent of IECA consultants work with low-income students for free each year. Many high school counselors have a caseload of several hundred students, and they have very little time to visit colleges, meet with representatives, or research trends in admissions—all of which an IEC is sure to do.

Parents are deeply invested in their children's success and happiness, and those who are willing to stretch financially in service of these goals often find that working with an IEC or hiring a tutor adds value. Parents may also invest money or time in helping their child to achieve on the athletic field or in the arts. Whether it is a travel team, camp, or private sports or music lessons, many parents fund activities with an eye on how they will look on the college application. But it's important for parents to realize that these are not mandatory expenses on the path to college. There are many artistic and athletic endeavors that can be pursued cheaply, and there are free tutoring resources online and at most high schools. Students don't need to spend a lot of money to build their Success Profile, and they can refer to Chapter Ten for a discussion of ways to avoid overspending.

OUR FASCINATION WITH COLLEGE RANKINGS

People love rankings. We buy highly rated cars and the top-ranked vacuum cleaners from *Consumer Reports*, watch the number-one box-office smash of the weekend, and snap up books on the bestseller list. These items are easy to rank based on sales figures or product characteristics. A college education is more subjective and personal, and it's difficult to quantify. Yet when *U.S. News & World Report* magazine released its first college rankings in 1983, it hit a bonanza. The yearly rankings publication became so popular that it has survived long after the magazine itself folded. *U.S. News* now has additional rankings for Best Value Colleges and Up and Coming Schools, as well as regional and major-specific rankings. In fact, it has morphed into an entire rankings business that now includes graduate schools, high schools, hospitals, law firms, vacations, retirement plans, nursing homes, mutual funds, and cars and trucks.

Despite its popularity, there is a major problem with the *U.S. News* college rankings: although it is seen as an indication of the quality of the education, in fact it has very little to do with what actually happens on campus. Almost 25 percent of the ranking determination is based on a reputational measure, in which college administrators are asked to rank other colleges, even institutions that they know nothing about. Other measures include alumni giving rates, student admissions selectivity, and the financial resources of the college. While the ranking does consider graduation and retention rates, it includes few other criteria measuring what actually happens to a student while on campus.

Despite this, the *U.S. News* rankings are read by millions of people, including alumni, hiring managers, and prospective students, who shape their views of the colleges through the rankings. The *U.S. News* rankings are so important to colleges that many of them make administrative decisions based on how those decisions will affect their rankings. Admissions policies such as Early Decision and "score choice" (the option to choose among SAT scores from multiple test dates to build one "super score" featuring a student's best scores in each test section) are among several initiatives that colleges have used to increase their standing in the *U.S. News* rankings. The use of the super score allows colleges to accept students with lower SAT scores without hurting the reported average of the freshman class. The Early Decision policy asks students to commit to a college during the application phase, which greatly increases the college's yield, a big factor in *U.S. News* rankings. For example, Duke University admitted 47 percent of its freshman class under its binding Early Decision program. Because these students have agreed to attend Duke, the yield, or percentage of admitted students who chose Duke, is increased.

Many colleges try to increase their number of applicants by hiring marketing firms, waiving application fees, or joining the Common Application, which allows students to apply to additional colleges with only a few extra clicks of the mouse. Colleges also buy targeted student mailing lists and travel across the world, visiting hundreds of schools to meet with thousands of prospective students, whose applications they promptly reject, thereby enhancing their *U.S. News* ranking.

In 2011, during the month that college rankings were released, the *U.S. News* website had ten million visitors, quite a lot of traffic for a defunct magazine site. With attention like that, it's no surprise that colleges adjust policies to improve their ranking. Some, such as Bucknell, Claremont McKenna,

George Washington, and Emory, have even admitted to falsifying freshmen statistics, and insiders speculate that many other colleges have adjusted data to benefit the rankings.[20] Not only is the rating game a business venture for the news outlets that compile the lists, but rankings are also, unfortunately, taken as a report card for the colleges themselves.

Other news sources have issued their own successful rankings of colleges. Readers can now look to the *Wall Street Journal, Forbes, Kiplinger's,* the *Times* of London, *Washington Monthly,* and even *Playboy* to see American colleges ranked in one way or another. In addition, PayScale ranks colleges by graduates' self-reported salaries, and LinkedIn has a ranking system that examines which colleges have the most employees at top firms within various industries.

The Obama Administration reacted to concerns over college cost and quality by discussing a plan to launch a government ranking of colleges based on value and affordability. These ratings would be tied to the 150 billion dollars in financial aid that the government gives each year. At the time of writing, this plan is still in the idea stage, but critics are concerned that tying rankings to university funding could encourage dishonesty and a focus of resources toward factors that improve rankings, rather than toward the quality of the academic programs.

Forbes has the only ranking system that is worthwhile for prospective families to review. It distinguishes itself by focusing on the "outputs" of college, rather than the "inputs." *Forbes* isn't concerned with selectivity, alumni giving, or what other college presidents think of a particular college. The *Forbes* ranking is focused entirely on what matters: what students are getting out of the college experience. *Forbes* partnered with the Center for College Affordability and Productivity to provide data that helps families explore concerns about debt levels, academic success, and future job prospects.

The *Forbes* rankings are focused on five areas: the success of graduates, student satisfaction, student debt levels, graduation rates, and receipt of competitive awards such as the Fulbright or Rhodes scholarships. It considers retention and professor ratings to get a sense of the student experience and evaluates graduates' career success through PayScale listings (see page 177) and numbers of alumni who have made nationally known contributions or achievements. Although success can be found at any college or university, if you want to evaluate a college through a ranking system, *Forbes* is clearly the one to read.

THE FULL MAILBOX: WHEN COLLEGES COME AFTER YOU

High school students' mailboxes are packed with college recruiting mail. They get brochures, emails, and offers of waived application fees. While this mail is often from lower-ranking or "up and coming" colleges, sometimes it is from well-known, selective colleges. This recruitment leaves students wondering, "Does this mean I'm in?"

In short: No, it doesn't mean that the college will accept you. Colleges have a long history of buying student information from the College Board for marketing purposes. They can focus their search on students with a certain SAT range, a certain GPA, or a particular state of residence. Critics of this practice say that selective colleges often market themselves to groups of students who don't meet their profile level, so that they can deny them. Thus, the college's acceptance rate drops, which is impressive to ranking guides, alumni, and other applicants, thereby leading to more applications, more rejections, higher rankings, and the continuation of the cycle. Students who get denied after receiving marketing mail can be left feeling like pawns in the ratings game.

Recently, colleges have begun to get more specific with the data in a practice called "microtargeting" (also employed by political campaigns and advertisers). Colleges can go beyond the search for grades and test scores and also use household income, or zip codes, which can be a reliable approximation of income levels. Despite the availability of financial aid, colleges have to consider the financial health of their own campus and remain focused on recruiting students who can pay the tuition without institutional aid. A research and consulting firm called Eduventures estimated that the admissions offices at four-year colleges spend about $2,500 per enrollee on recruitment office and marketing costs, with mail contact occurring an average of 6.6 times per student.[21]

Although microtargeting has attracted criticism, it's important to note that many colleges do use it to encourage high-performing low-income students to apply to their colleges, and that this outreach is crucial to maintaining an economically diverse student body.

Recruiting brochures from selective colleges do not make up the majority of the mail that a typical student receives. Hundreds of less selective colleges use recruiting mailings as a means to spread the word about their college and to enroll more students. Their mailings may inform students about programs offered, support services, internship or extracurricular offerings, class sizes, or freshman seminar topics. Despite all the attention on selective schools, fewer than 100 colleges have an acceptance rate lower than 25 percent.[22] Fortunately, there are more than five hundred four-year colleges, including some popular state universities and private liberal-arts colleges, that accept 75 percent or more of their applicants. There are also hundreds of universities that are open-admission. A motivated student who develops her Success Profile will find it possible to excel at any of them.

The mystique about college admissions is fueled by a

belief in top colleges' long history of excellence and their ability to offer an educational opportunity that simply cannot be had at one of the hundreds of less selective colleges. However, as the next chapter will reveal, success is not dependent on the college attended. It's time to loosen the stranglehold that elite colleges have on the minds and bank accounts of students and parents, and to begin to examine the real secrets to college and career success.

I am very sorry to inform you that it is not possible to offer you admission to the Class of 2013...

Over twenty-nine thousand students, a record number, applied to the entering class...

Past experience suggests that the particular college a student attends is far less important than what the student does to develop his or her strengths and talents over the next four years...

We very much appreciate the interest you have shown in Harvard College. We hope that you will accept the best wishes of the Committee for success in all your future endeavors.

Harvard College

Examining the Link between
Top Colleges and Success

There are many ways to define success, and each individual will have a different view of what makes a successful life. Most of us would name health, happiness, and good relationships with people as markers of success. We might also include personal fulfillment, contributing to society, financial security, power and influence, and advancement in a career of choice. Whatever our definition of success, we tend to be willing to sacrifice or work hard in order to ensure a positive future. Attending an elite college is supposed to be the first decisive step on the path to happiness and success. But as I have hinted before, attending a top college may not really have an important role in helping the graduate find lifelong success.

ELITE COLLEGES AND HAPPINESS

The more idealistic among us imagine college as a time of immense personal and intellectual development, and think that the choice of school matters a great deal because the "right" (usually elite) school will offer an atmosphere that supports students' exploration and personal growth better than any other could. College is supposed to have the perfect mix of people with whom to make lasting friendships, and to foster an increased level of knowledge and thoughtfulness that sticks with graduates for good. Others might assume that graduates of elite colleges will have more career success and better career options, which will lead to happiness and fulfillment in other areas of life. But a recent study found no correlation whatsoever between attending a prestigious college and reporting well-being and engagement in work later in life.

The May 2014 study of almost thirty thousand college graduates is the largest of its kind. It was conducted by Gallup pollsters and Purdue University. The participants lived in all fifty states and attended a variety of colleges, including Ivy League schools, state universities, and small liberal-arts schools of all levels of selectivity. Doing their best to quantify happiness, the researchers asked adults a variety of background questions focused on two key areas:

Participants' engagement with their current work, meaning job satisfaction, feeling connected with their organizations, liking what they do and feeling they do it well, and having someone who cares about them at work.[23]

Participants' well-being, which was further divided into five kinds of well-being: a sense of purpose, social well-being, financial well-being, a sense of community, and physical well-being (health).[24]

The surprising finding was that the people who attended selective colleges were no better off in any of these measured areas than those who attended any other type of college. According to the poll, about 39 percent of all college graduates experience engagement at work, and there is no difference in engagement between graduates of top-100 *U.S. News & World Report* schools and graduates of other institutions. Similarly, 11 percent of all college graduates report that they are "thriving" in all five elements of well-being, and the percentage of people in that coveted position is no larger for graduates of the top-ranked 100 schools than for others. (However, being engaged at work makes it five times more likely that a participant will be thriving across the board.)[25]

The study did find specific factors that increased the graduates' odds of reporting being engaged at work or experiencing high levels of well-being. Participants who had a mentor at college, or a professor who supported and encouraged them, were twice as likely to report being engaged at work. Similarly, those who had participated in deep learning, such as internships, long papers or projects, or extensive extracurricular involvement, while in college were also twice as likely to report being engaged at work. Supportive, encouraging mentors and opportunities for intensive, challenging projects are not the sole domain of elite colleges. In fact, any student at any university can pursue these relationships and opportunities for himself. The study also found that the odds of thriving in all areas of well-being were twice as likely for graduates who felt emotionally attached to their colleges. Clearly, the relationship between a student's campus experience and her future well-being is what matters, not the specific college she attended. The worst news was for graduates with student-loan debt, who reported low levels of well-being and were shown to be risk-averse. Only 2 percent of graduates with $20,000 to $40,000 in debt reported themselves as "thriving." That is a striking statistic when you consider that over 70 percent of college seniors now have student-loan debt, with the average amount over $33,000.[26]

Overall, the survey showed that things correlated with success (defined as workplace engagement and overall well-being) were low student-loan debt, quality relationships with professors, deep learning, and active involvement at college. Fortunately, none of that has to be left to chance, and none of it depends on getting admitted to a particular school.

ELITE COLLEGES AND FINANCIAL SUCCESS

So much for happiness. But elite colleges are at least able to ensure graduates' financial and career success, right? Economists Alan Krueger and Stacy Dale published a study shattering that myth. They found that students with high test scores who were motivated enough to apply to selective colleges went on to achieve earnings similar to the earnings of those who actually attended elite colleges. Even students who were *rejected* from elite colleges earned as much as those who attended!

The counterintuitive, provocative conclusions of their study are strong evidence that the student, not the college, is most responsible for attaining a successful career.

Alan Krueger is a top economist who was recently named chairman of the White House Council of Economic Advisers by President Obama. He also served as the US Assistant Secretary of the Treasury in the Obama administration. He and his coauthor can hardly be accused of an anti-elite bias: Dale graduated from Princeton, and Krueger is a graduate of two elite colleges, Cornell and Harvard, and is a professor of economics at Princeton.

The study, part I

Krueger and Dale's first study, called "Estimating the Payoff to Attending a More Selective College," reviewed earnings data from the College and Beyond Survey, which was completed by more than 14,000 students who attended 27 different colleges.[27] Some of the colleges were elite, such as Stanford, Georgetown, Duke, Rice, Princeton, and the University of Pennsylvania. Others colleges in the study were at the middle level, moderately selective in admissions, such as Xavier, Penn State, Miami of Ohio, and Tulane. Note that the study did not include graduates of lower-ranked colleges or state colleges that are not the flagship campus in their state. It is an exhaustive study comparing the incomes of high-achieving students who attended elite colleges and the incomes of those who were accepted to elite colleges but chose to attend middle-ranked colleges.

Looking at the raw data, it is easy to see why we believe that top colleges enhance their graduates' earnings. According to the College and Beyond Survey, the average student who entered a highly selective college (e.g., Princeton, Swarthmore, or the University of Pennsylvania) in 1976 earned $92,000 in 1995. The average graduate from a moderately selective college (e.g., Penn State, Denison, or Tulane), earned $70,000—a whopping $22,000 less.

Krueger and Dale saw a problem with this comparison: Students who attend elite colleges may be likely to have higher earnings regardless of where they attend college for the same reasons that they were admitted to the selective colleges in the first place. The personal qualities and achievements that lead admissions committees to select certain applicants for admission are the same qualities that are likely to be rewarded in the labor market (and the same qualities that make up the Success Profile, described on page 59–64).

To compensate for the problem, Krueger and Dale focused their study on high-achieving students who applied to and were accepted by both elite and middle-ranked colleges. Some students chose to attend the elite colleges and others turned them down for middle-ranked colleges.

Krueger noted in the study, "Our research found that earnings were unrelated to the selectivity of the college that students had attended among those who had comparable options. For example, the average earnings for the 519 students who were accepted by both moderately selective . . . and highly selective schools . . . varied little, no matter which type of college they attended." Thus, the student who was accepted to Princeton and Tulane in 1976, but elected to attend Tulane, had the same earnings as a student who graduated from Princeton, rather than matching up with Tulane graduates who were not accepted to elite colleges (and earned less).

Along with being accepted to top colleges (whether or not they attended), there are a few things these students likely had in common: They were smart, motivated, and ambitious, and twenty years later, their average earnings benefitted from it. Those who chose middle-ranked schools may have done so for any number of reasons, such as merit scholarships, distance from home, or specific academic opportunities, but the results prove their decision was not a mistake.

The study was completed over ten years before this writing, but its findings are especially relevant today, as elite colleges have become even more selective and the student debt level has surpassed one trillion dollars. Families weigh the high price of tuition against the payoffs they see down the road: they subscribe to the rationale that students who attend more selective colleges get better jobs and have higher earnings throughout their careers. They feel that students benefit from highly regarded professors, bright classmates, strong campus career-services offices, and potentially a nod from future employers for having a big-name college on the resume. These families are willing to take on sometimes crippling debt for better potential economic opportunities. If your family is currently considering such a tradeoff, I urge you to consider the implications of this study.

The study, part II

In 2011, after updating their study and expanding its parameters, Krueger and Dale found similar results again. They tracked their 1976 cohort's earnings from 1983 to 2007. They also followed the earnings from 1993 to 2007 of a new cohort of students, who started college in 1989.[28]

The new study added one additional dimension and found remarkable results. The researchers asked the graduates to list all of the colleges they had applied to and the corresponding admissions decisions. They found that students with high SAT scores had comparable earnings, no matter where they went to college. For example, graduates who scored above 1400 on the SAT and went to Duke had the same average salary as other over-1400 scorers who went to Denison. Even students who were rejected by Duke and attended Denison had similar earnings to Duke grads', as long as they had a comparably high SAT score and the initiative to apply to elite colleges. The better predictor of earnings in this study was the average SAT score of the most selective school the student *applied to*, not the average SAT score of the college he graduated from.

The Steven Spielberg Effect

Krueger and Dale conclude that where a student applies to college offers some insight into his ambition and may be the best predictor of his future success. They cite the "Steven Spielberg Effect," a reference to one of the top movie producers of all time. Spielberg applied to USC and UCLA, two of the top undergraduate film schools in the country, and was rejected. He instead attended Cal State Long Beach, and he went on to tremendous success in his field.

Krueger suggests, "It appears that student ambition, as reflected in the quality of the school to which he or she applies, is a better predictor of earning success than what college they ultimately choose or which college chooses them."[29]

Elite colleges do matter for some groups

The Krueger and Dale study has one large caveat: their research did not show the same results for black, Latino, and low-income students, or those whose parents did not have a bachelor's degree. For these students, attending a higher-ranking college did positively influence later earnings. High-achieving minority students and first-generation college students saw a significant increase in salary for attending elite colleges. Based on this finding, Krueger offered this advice to elite colleges: "Recognize that the most disadvantaged students benefit most from your instruction. Set financial aid and admission policies accordingly."[30]

We can assume that something about their elite college experience was important to these students' career opportunities, even when it was not important to the majority of people in the study. It's possible that their parents did not have connections that could lead to jobs for their children. They may not have been able to offer their children advice about internships, career choice, or interview tips, or to relate their own experience in these areas. But this is not to say that elite colleges are the only path to success for minority, low-income, and first-generation college students. A student at any college can take charge of his education, build relationships with professors and students, develop skills, and have meaningful academic gains and professional internships. On page 59, students can learn about how to develop their Success Profile, build networks, and gain experiences that are valuable in the job market.

ELITE COLLEGES AND BUSINESS SUCCESS

It might not be surprising that a selection of "average" people would find that their alma mater didn't contribute much to their later success. But for real superstars in society, we feel more confident that they went to top colleges. We know that many elite college graduates are represented in the management teams at investment banks and top law firms. The last four United States presidents each had at least one Ivy League degree. It seems safe to conclude that the top of the business world is dominated by graduates of elite colleges.

However, if you look at the table of where the CEOs of the Standard & Poor 500 companies went to college, you find a wide breadth of colleges represented. Would you be surprised to know that more CEOs of S&P 500 companies went to Rutgers than to Brown, Duke, and Columbia combined? While Harvard and Cornell take the top two spots, the rest of the top thirteen includes seven state universities. Seven of the CEOs didn't even graduate from college at all. It would be hard to conclude, after looking at this table, that graduating from an elite college was an important step to the CEO suite.

Colleges producing the most CEOs of companies in the S&P 500

COLLEGE	NUMBER OF CEOS
Harvard	14
Cornell	10
University of Texas System	9
Penn State	8
Rutgers	8
Stanford	8
Princeton	7
Dartmouth	6
Indiana	6
Michigan	6
Purdue	6
Missouri	6
Yale	6
Brown	5
Holy Cross	5
Miami University (Ohio)	5
Notre Dame	5

Table Continues

COLLEGE	NUMBER OF CEOS
Texas A&M	5
University of California, Berkeley	5
Wisconsin	5
Colgate	4
Colorado School of Mines	4
LSU	4
MIT	4
UCLA	4
Colorado	4
Virginia	4

Table represents number of CEOs of companies in the S&P 500 index who received an undergraduate degree from each college or university. Data excludes twenty-six CEOs for whom no information is available. Seven CEOs were identified as not having graduated from an undergraduate institution.

Schools producing three CEOs include Boston College, Bucknell, Georgia Tech, Kettering University, Lehigh, Ohio University, Rensselaer, Southern Methodist, Ohio State, Iowa, University of North Carolina, University of Pennsylvania, University of Southern California, Villanova, Wake Forest, and Wellesley.

Source: S&P Capital IQ, Darien Academic Advisors. Data as of September 30, 2014.

ELITE COLLEGES COLLECT SUCCESSFUL PEOPLE— THEY DON'T MAKE THEM

Bill Gates, the founder of Microsoft, and Mark Zuckerberg, the founder of Facebook, famously dropped out of Harvard to start their companies. Clearly, their success was not related to having a Harvard diploma, since they never received one. They were already bright, ambitious achievers when they applied to Harvard, and the admissions committee recognized this and accepted them. Harvard was only one expensive stop on the path to success that was already in the works. But what if they had stayed and graduated from Harvard? We would likely conclude that Harvard had launched them to successful careers. It would be another false piece of evidence indicating that attending an elite college will increase your odds of success.

Elite colleges reject about 90 percent of the students who apply. In the 10 percent they do accept, admissions committees are looking for signs of grit, motivation, and intellectual prowess. They accept students who not only have potential, but who have already exhibited it through extraordinary achievement and initiative. These students are brought together as a freshman class, and then, four years later, let loose on the world. Is it any surprise that many of them continue to be successful? It might not be correct to assume that during those four years something magical happened that led to postgraduate success, when it is likely that these people would be successful no matter where they went to college.

The truth is that for most strong high school students, it is unlikely that the name on your diploma will have any influence whatsoever on your personal success. It doesn't provide an increase in earnings or happiness, and it isn't related to graduate-school acceptance either. Top graduate schools like Harvard accept students from hundreds of different colleges, placing the focus on grades, testing, and accomplishments rather than on the name of the undergraduate institution. Despite the intensity of the college admissions process, the years of shaping yourself into a desirable applicant, and the expense of private universities, your future earnings are likely to be the same whether you go to an elite college or a moderately selective one. Success and top colleges are not linked in the way that most people think they are.

WHY DOES ATTENDING AN ELITE COLLEGE HAVE NO IMPACT ON EARNINGS FOR TOP STUDENTS?

Several factors may explain why the degree of college selectivity has little impact on salary and earnings for high-achieving students. Certainly we might conclude that the student's motivation, intelligence, and hard work are the main factors in success. Alan Krueger gave *The New York Times* this advice for students: "Don't believe that the only school worth attending is one that would not admit you. That you go to college is more important than where you go. Find a school whose academic strengths match your interests and that devotes resources to instruction in those fields. Recognize that your own motivation, ambition and talents will determine your success more than the college name on your diploma."[31]

ISAAC KINDE, DNA SEQUENCING RESEARCHER

 People really can turn down Stanford and not only live to tell about it, but go on to great success. Isaac Kinde and his fellow researchers are working to create new techniques to improve the accuracy of DNA sequencing. They hope to detect cancers of the colon, pancreas, and ovaries earlier and with more efficiency. The work that Isaac and his team have done has been published in scientific journals such as *Nature, Science Translational Medicine*, and *PLOS ONE*.

Isaac was a top high school student from San Bernadino, California, who was accepted at Stanford but chose to attend the University of Maryland-Baltimore County (UMBC) and its well-regarded Meyerhoff Scholars Program. Isaac explains, "I chose UMBC because of the Meyerhoff Program, which provides support and mentoring for individuals interested in pursuing careers in science. The offered mentorship was a crucial determinant for me because I think it is easy to get lost in college. Further, it is through this program that I connected with my undergraduate

research mentor—Dr. Michael Summers—who provided the guidance and encouragement that
ultimately prepared me exceptionally well for an MD-
PhD program."

Isaac had a great experience at UMBC, calling it
"life-changing." He reports, "It has been an incredible journey filled with both struggle and exhilaration." Isaac will soon be graduating with an MD and
PhD from Johns Hopkins University School of Medicine, and in the future, we will probably be reading
great things about his continuing research and medical career in pathology.

This advice aligns with the message at the heart of this
book: that success is within a person's own power and will
not be determined by the college she attends. Many students
of today are tenaciously working to be one of the 5 or 10
percent accepted by an elite college, but typically that process ends with disappointment—these colleges are called
"selective" for a reason! It's sad to see students become fa-
tigued or lose confidence over elite college admissions when
studies show that it means so little in the long run.

We can also consider that perhaps the name brand of the
undergraduate college does not mean as much to hiring employers as we thought that it did. In some fields and for some
hiring managers, the name of the college is not relevant. For
others, hiring managers might look more closely at the name
and quality of the graduate program, which may be more
relevant to the chosen career. Or perhaps the luster of the
elite college degree on the resume wears off after the graduates' first few years in the workforce.

A recent Gallup poll shows conflicting opinions between
the American public and business leaders when considering
the importance of the college attended by the applicant in the

hiring process. The survey of 623 business leaders showed that only 9 percent of them rated "where a candidate received his or her college degree" as "very important," and 54 percent rated it as "not very important" or "not at all important." However, when 1,000 United States citizens were polled, 30 percent of them said that where a job candidate received his or her degree was "very important" and only 20 percent rated it as "not very important" or "not at all important."[32] The business leaders' focus was on knowledge and applied skills, with 84 percent rating the candidate's "amount of knowledge in the field" as very important, and 79 percent viewing the candidate's applied skills in the field as very important.

We can also look at students' academic performance while they are at college. All young people are on a journey, and sometimes even students at elite colleges decide to focus more on parties than on their academics, while their counterpart at a middle-tier school may decide that he does not have the luxury of slacking off. These students' college GPAs and transcripts will make the distinction clear to hiring managers, who may be more inclined to hire the harder-working student. Involvement in on-campus activities, work experience in paid jobs or internships, and cultivation of professional relationships are additional areas of focus for motivated students, which slackers often ignore—again, regardless of the schools they attend.

IS IT BETTER TO BE A BIG FISH IN A LITTLE POND?

Another important point is that the high-achieving student who attends a middle-tier school may be more likely to be at the top of his class. He may graduate with a higher GPA, higher class rank, or more opportunities to work with professors. He may get more attention from hiring managers because of his top standing in his class and his high grades. For some students, selecting a college where they are likely to be in the top third at graduation is a good choice.

The student who turns down Columbia University to attend Ohio State may do so to save money, but she could end up with an added benefit. The Krueger and Dale study found that high-achieving students who went to middle-range colleges tended to have a higher class rank than their peers who went to elite colleges.[33] I have known students who transferred out of rigorous and competitive high schools to enroll in more nurturing schools with a mix of student ability levels. They thrived there and felt invigorated by being at the head of the class, rather than struggling to stay in the middle. The Big Fish–Little Pond theory is about more than just having less competition. It suggests that the people around us affect how we learn, and that we evaluate ourselves relative to others in the class.

If you were to sit in on an organic chemistry class at MIT, you would probably hear an entirely different discussion than you would in the organic chemistry class at Florida State. Students would ask different questions, and the professor would spend time on concepts that are of interest to the group she is teaching. As a result, a student in the MIT class may consider herself to be an average chemistry student because of her perception of her peers, when at a lower-ranked college, she might consider herself to be strong in chemistry.

Malcolm Gladwell showcased the Big Fish–Little Pond theory in his book *David and Goliath*, in which he observed the graduation rates of students interested in science, technology, engineering, and math (STEM) careers.[34] STEM careers are hot right now, offering some of the highest-paying jobs for college graduates. Gladwell cites studies that showed that it was the "big fish" who dominated in receiving STEM degrees, no matter what type of college they attended.

The students with the highest incoming SAT scores (i.e.,

the big fish) were the ones who stuck with STEM classes, while those whose SAT scores were at the lower end for their college dropped out at a higher rate. For example, at Hartwick, a less selective college, 55 percent of the STEM degrees were awarded to the one-third of the class that had the highest incoming SAT score. That group averaged a 562 on the math SAT and went on to get more than half of Hartwick's STEM degrees. At Harvard, similarly, it was the top third of the class who earned 53 percent of the STEM degrees. This group of students had a 753 average on the math SAT.[35]

But what is interesting to consider is the results of the lowest-scoring group of Harvard students. Their average math SAT was a 581, which was higher than the top group's at Hartwick. However, at Harvard, this group didn't stay in STEM at a high rate; only 15 percent of them finished a STEM degree. This makes the case that if you are a student who hopes to succeed in a STEM major, you might increase your odds by enrolling in a college where your math abilities are in the top one-third of the class.

Gladwell cited research by Michael Chang of the University of California, who found that "the likelihood of someone completing a STEM degree—all things being equal—rises by 2 percentage points for every 10-point decrease in the university's average SAT score."[36]

Why might that be? Consider an example: Henry was a student at MIT who had graduated first in his class in high school. During his sophomore year, he was eager to take on the challenges of organic chemistry, but he found it difficult from the start. He did not ask questions frequently, since no one else seemed to be as perplexed as he was. When he did ask a question, he would nod and pretend to understand, and to avoid slowing the group down, he didn't ask follow-up questions. It wasn't long before Henry had to drop organic chemistry.

Because he was intent on a career in medicine, Henry

arranged to retake organic chemistry during the summer session at Florida State. He was more successful in his second attempt at the material, partly because of his surroundings. When he asked questions, others listened and asked follow-up questions. Henry felt that he was one of the stronger students in the class; that he was really getting it. This encouraged him to persevere when things got hard.

Little fish can do well, too

Studies such as those mentioned in this chapter help to change the conversation about education and help people to see different possibilities and different paths to success. The conclusions drawn may not offer a one-size-fits-all solution. Although the studies make good points, it is important to point out that the conclusions may not apply to all students. For example, personalities are different, and some students truly thrive in competitive environments. They might not put forth a full effort without peers who are perceived as a step ahead of them, or they might learn more from the insights of those who have a better understanding of the material. Students have the ability to succeed no matter where they go to college, but they should also consider their own strengths, learning styles, and preferences as they make decisions.

CAMPUS RECRUITING BY FINANCE, CONSULTING, AND OTHER SELECTIVE FIRMS

The biggest doubters of the theory that attending an elite college will not affect your future earnings are those who hope to work on Wall Street or at consulting or other selective firms. They cite the common belief that these firms only recruit at elite colleges, so those attending the majority of universities are out of luck.

While it is true that investment banks and consulting firms have "target schools" where they focus more of their recruiting attention, this is not their only hiring pool. Their incoming analyst and summer intern programs typically include several students who were hired outside the campus-visit and recruiting sessions. These students may have had connections with people at the firm who helped them get a job, or they may have simply applied online and been selected based on their resume, high SAT score, and credentials.

McKinsey & Company, a prestigious consulting firm, indicates on its website that besides the elite private colleges, it does campus interviewing at the Universities of Michigan, North Carolina, California, and Texas, as well as at Georgia Tech. It also states, "McKinsey interviews candidates from a variety of undergraduate sources, including large state colleges and universities and smaller private institutions. Even if we are unable to come in person to your campus, we are still interested in reviewing your application."

Goldman Sachs recruits at many top colleges, but has also recently visited campuses and hired employees from Spelman, Villanova, Carnegie Mellon, and Brigham Young University.

Let's face it: getting hired by a top firm is difficult, no matter where you go to college. The reality is that most students get their first jobs outside the campus recruiting process. No matter what college you graduate from, you have to be aggressive and ambitious in your job search. Keep in mind that starting at less popular firms and building up your experience and skills is an effective way to get to the top in your field. See page 120 for more suggestions on job hunting.

RECRUITING AT GOOGLE

A *CNN/Money* survey of college students around the world found that a job at Google is the most sought-after position for new college graduates.[37] Google is an innovative global technology leader headquartered in Mountain View, California, with more than 46,000 employees. Two million people per year submit resumes to Google, hoping to land one of about one thousand new positions annually.[38] Candidates are rated on their leadership potential, their knowledge, their humility, and how they think. As the Google website says, "Googlers are people who want to do cool things that matter."

What candidates *aren't* rated on is the selectivity of the college they attended. Very little focus is paid even to the grades earned. Google is at the forefront of a trend toward evaluating applicants based on their skills and potential, rather than their pedigree.

Laszlo Bock, the senior vice president of people operations for Google, explained to *The New York Times*, "Your college degree is not a proxy anymore for having the skills or traits to do any job."[39] He indicated that Google is looking for general cognitive ability, such as the ability to think on your feet, to pull together bits of information into one theme, and to learn and adapt to an ever-changing field.

Bock told *The New York Times* that GPAs and test scores are both "worthless" hiring criteria. He went on to discuss Google's main hiring attributes, which include:

- coding ability for technology roles (which are half of Google positions)
- general cognitive ability (not IQ, but the ability to learn or to process information on the fly)

▶ emergent leadership (knowing when to lead and
   when to follow)
▶ humility and ownership (the ability to accept other
   people's ideas when they are better)[40]

Working on a team (see page 116) or holding a part-time
job or internship (see page 112) while in school might help
you develop these qualities. When asked again about GPAs,
Bock conceded, "Grades certainly don't hurt." If an applicant's grades reflect real skills that she can apply on the job,
then that is valuable to Google, or any firm.[41]

Bock's advice for college students is: "Make sure that
you're getting out of it not only a broadening of your knowledge, but skills that will be valued in today's workplace."[42]
This is a warning not to relax during college and expect to
thrive in the current economy because of your college degree. It's important to develop skills and strengths in college,
and that might not happen without extra effort on your part.

PARISA TABRIZ, SECURITY PRINCESS

 Parisa Tabriz has an enviable job at one of
the hottest companies in the world. She is
the "security princess" at Google (that is
the actual title of her job), head of the information security engineering team. Parisa is responsible for
improving Google's product security by conducting
security-design and code reviews, and by building
and enhancing Google technology. In simple terms,
she protects Google users from cybercrime.

You might expect a person who made it to this senior role at Google in her twenties to have come from
Stanford or Caltech. But Parisa went to the University

of Illinois. She was drawn to the school for its strong engineering program and in-state tuition. When asked by news source "60 Second Recap" if she would do it all over again, she answered, "Yep! University of Illinois has a world-class college of engineering. Studying in an environment that exposed and gave me access to incredible resources (people, research projects, labs, equipment) is a huge reason I had the career opportunities I did. I graduated without any debt."[43]

Parisa started out as an engineering student, but she found her passion for computer science not in an academic class, but in a casual student club. She was one of the only women in a group of computer science students who met on Friday nights to learn about web security. They tried new ideas and learned from one another. Her experience with this group launched her career, and Parisa is now one of the world's experts on Internet security.[44]

Realities of College Life Today

In many countries throughout the world, college students live with their parents and commute to classes each day. The main focuses of the college experience are the academics, the credential, and preparation for career and adulthood. But in the United States, college has come to be seen as a rite of passage or a life-changing journey. That journey is interpreted differently by different people: some see college as a trial of independent living, and others think of it as a time to have fun before the real world beckons, or to make deep and lasting friendships. Certainly, it is a time to try new things, live and work with a diverse group of people, improve academic and social skills, prepare for a career, and shape your adult identity. We all have different values and priorities, so our views of the purpose of a college education differ. But we can all agree that when a young person goes to college, he is part of an educational experience that encompasses much more than academics.

Still, once you get past the mystique of American universities and begin to peel back the layers, you will see that colleges are not the temples of learning and training grounds for adulthood that we like to imagine. From Ivies to nonselective colleges, schools are rife with potential problems, such as:

▶ **Decline in student engagement:** Students spend less time studying than they did in the past, are on social media extensively, don't attend class frequently, and rarely meet personally with a professor.

▶ **Lack of academic progress:** Studies show little to no gains in critical thought and complex problem-solving skills during a student's time in college.

▶ **Academic Dishonesty:** Fifty-five percent of college presidents say that plagiarism in students' papers has increased over the past 10 years. Among those who have seen an increase in plagiarism, 89 percent say computers and the Internet have played a major role.[45]

▶ **Social stress:** The party culture, the fraternity and sorority rushing process, and navigating an "around-the-clock" life with peers leaves students encountering new pressures and stress.

▶ **Mental health and depression on campus:** Some students leave college or are unhappy because of general malaise or a lack of purpose. The American Psychological Association reports that depression among college students has increased 10 percent over the last ten years. There are more than 1,100 suicides each year on college campuses.

▶ **Sexual assaults:** The federal government is investigating 55 colleges for wrongly handling sexual assault accusations.

▶ **Alcohol abuse:** One-third of college students report being drunk three or more times a month, and 44 percent report frequent binge drinking.

▶ **Financial distress:** Parents and students are taking on debt and paying more than they can afford for college tuition and other fees.

▶ **Post-graduation woes:** Many new college graduates have trouble finding meaningful employment, and only 27 percent find jobs related to their majors.[46]

I'm not suggesting that you skip college, but it's important for parents and students to go into the college environment with an understanding of potential pitfalls, and to develop a plan for success. It's clear that colleges are failing us in many ways. You cannot sit back and expect a college to deliver an educational experience that will prepare you for the rest of your life. You need to take matters into your own hands and be sure that you're developing the skills that you need for success, building meaningful relationships, and taking care of yourself. Let's explore a few of the above issues in more depth.

EMOTIONAL HEALTH AND THE HEDONISTIC PARTY CULTURE

When students evaluate colleges, they look for a "good fit." Of course this "fit" has an academic component, but it also involves factors that have nothing to do with coursework or majors. The climate, location, presence or lack of fraternities and sororities, male-female ratio, athletics, and campus amenities are common decision points. Although college is about so much more than academics, we must acknowledge that academics are the primary reason that students are there. Yet, if you consider the problems on campuses, it's easy to see that not all students make academics their primary focus.

I don't need to describe the college party culture, because it has seeped into the movies, the news, and the consciousness of teenagers and their parents. To be sure, there are wild parties, excessive drinking, and experimentation in which students may or may not participate. If they do, maybe they'll learn from it, maybe they'll enjoy it, and maybe it will cause them despair.

Emergency rooms near college campuses admit intoxicated patients who need medical intervention due to alcohol poisoning or injury. Drunken college students have been known to fall from windows and porches, wander off, and even drown. Drinking often plays a role in sexual assault cases and can also lead to depression.

We don't know if sexual assaults have increased on campus, since it is thought that most go unreported. Fifty-five colleges, including Ivy League institutions, state universities, and liberal arts colleges, are facing federal investigations for the way they have handled sexual abuse allegations. These investigations are prompting all colleges to review their policies and improve practices for investigating sexual assault accusations, as well as beef up prevention programs for students.

Besides the obvious dangers from the party culture, it's also important to look at the leisure culture of college. Imagine sleeping until noon, then lounging in the sun, playing video games, scrolling through your Twitter feed, and enjoying time on the rock-climbing wall in between visits to a dining hall stocked with your favorite foods. Finish it off with a night out dancing or drinking with friends. Does this sound like a day at Club Med? It's actually a typical day on campus for many college students.

Excessive leisure time is a fact of college life. Students value resort-style leisure facilities, and some colleges compete with one another in developing amazing recreation centers that entice students to enroll. Texas Tech has an $8.4 million "lazy river ride," and LSU will soon one-up them with a lazy river opening in 2016 that will be shaped like the letters "LSU" in its signature font. University of Missouri has an indoor beach club with palm trees, a waterfall, and a Playboy Mansion–style grotto. There are 157 recreational capital projects in the works on college campuses, according to NIRSA: Leaders in Campus Recreation, with estimated costs of $1.7 billion.[47]

Daily life without structure is difficult for people of all ages. Students who are not working or involved on campus often feel a lack of purpose, which can lead to malaise, depression, or dropping out of college. Certainly there are many people who are very busy at college, and they would scoff at the "day in the life" description above. Those young adults are thriving at college and are likely to continue to thrive. But it's also important to realize that for many students, college is one long, expensive vacation from which they gain very little.

ARE THEY LEARNING ANYTHING?

The importance of intellectual life on campus is obvious. Students learn from professors and classmates and develop skills in many areas. Yet, as we heard from Laszlo Bock, the human resources manager at Google, the college degree alone will no longer open doors. It is not only the academic credential but also academic skills that are important to career success. Are students graduating from college with knowledge and skills that are greatly improved over the levels that they had attained when they graduated from high school? Even if recent college graduates don't remember specific formulas, facts, or histories, is it safe to conclude that they have learned how to think, analyze, and communicate better than when they left high school?

Richard Arum and Josipa Roksa authored a groundbreaking book, *Academically Adrift: Limited Learning on College Campuses*, which looks beyond grades and self-reported attitudes about college and measures what students learn and how they improve over the course of college. As you can guess from the title, they found that students aren't learning very much at all.

Arum and Roksa note that study time on campus

has decreased sharply. In 1961, the average student spent twenty-five hours per week studying. By 1981, the numbers had slipped, with the average student studying twenty hours per week, and by 2003, it was only thirteen hours per week. In fact, the college students in 2003 spent only twenty-eight hours weekly on all academic pursuits combined (including class), less than a typical high school student spends in class alone. Only 20 percent of college students today report studying more than twenty hours per week outside class.[48]

The rule of thumb that most professors recommend is two hours of preparation and study for each hour of class. Considering that most college students take a fifteen-hour weekly course load, that would imply thirty hours of studying and fifteen hours of class, making for a forty-five-hour academic work week. What we see instead is a twenty-eight-hour academic week, although some students don't attend class frequently and rarely study, and thus clock in far less time than this.

Curiously, this large decline in time spent on academics has had no negative effect on student GPAs. In fact, grade-point averages have gone up dramatically since the 1960s. Currently, 43 percent of college grades are As, while in 1960, only 15 percent of grades awarded were As. The 1960s were the days of the "gentleman's C," with 35 percent of college grades awarded in the C range. Today, a C represents fewer than 15 percent of grades awarded to college students.[49]

One might think that the young people of today must be a lot smarter than those of the 1960s, since they study less and get much better grades. But in reality, the college culture has changed and grade inflation has become the norm. Professors who are hard graders or give "too much" work find themselves with low marks on student evaluations and under-enrolled classes, while professors who put together a light, entertaining class and award many As will enjoy strong reviews and robust registration for their classes.

While we know that grades are inflated and students are studying far less than they used to, this doesn't tell us whether they have learned anything or made progress in developing skills that are needed in the workforce. One way to discover how much students are learning is to test them in these areas at the beginning of college, and then test them again in the middle and the end. For example, if you saved a persuasive writing essay from an incoming freshman and then asked him to write a similar response two or four years later, you would expect to see improvement not only in writing skills, but also in reasoning and critical thinking. The Collegiate Learning Assessment (CLA), discussed below, measures these skills and gives us insight into the level of academic progress.

MEASURING ACADEMIC PROGRESS WITH THE COLLEGIATE LEARNING ASSESSMENT (CLA)

The role of the university in preparing students for jobs has been questioned by business leaders, policy makers, journalists, and nervous parents. We read that students do not have the skills for the working world, and we are unsure whether high schools, colleges, students, or all three are to blame.

Even Derek Bok, former president of Harvard University, admits that "colleges and universities, for all the benefits they bring, accomplish far less for their students than they should." He explains that many college graduates are not meeting employers' expectations, either in their writing skills or in their ability to "reason clearly or perform competently in analyzing complex, non-technical problems."[50]

To further evaluate this, we can look at one up-and-coming measure of academic progress in college. The Collegiate

Learning Assessment (CLA) is a good measure of collegiate learning because it doesn't rely on self-reported opinions, but instead is an actual test that evaluates skills and measures improvement. It asks students to solve complex problems by using data and resources to analyze possibilities and convey their ideas.

The CLA is administered by the Council for Aid to Education and has been used by more than seven hundred colleges throughout the world. College administrators use it to measure how students at their college are growing academically and to compare that growth to other colleges or to norms. According to the CLA site, "Students today can no longer rely solely on mastery of discipline-based information. They need to be able to analyze and evaluate information, solve problems, and communicate effectively. Beyond just accumulating facts, they must be able to access, structure, and use information." This echoes the sentiment of many employers. The CLA exam features open-ended questions that measure a student's analytical reasoning, problem-solving, and writing skills.

CLA questions focus on real-world situations in which an issue, problem, or conflict is identified. Students have to address the issue, suggest a solution, or recommend a course of action. Rather than using personal opinions, they have access to a document library with six to twelve items, such as technical reports, data tables, newspaper articles, office memoranda, emails, and other everyday materials. They have sixty minutes to read the documents, analyze the problem, and recommend a solution.

The results of the CLA tests are kept private by the individual colleges and have not been published, so we have no idea how college students are doing on the test. However, Arum and Roksa conducted a study of 2,322 students at twenty-four colleges, monitoring their progress on the

CLA, with a focus on how much improvement they showed in critical thinking, complex reasoning, and writing. The result of the study forms the crux of their book *Academically Adrift*.

They found that 45 percent of these students showed no gain in critical thinking, complex reasoning, or writing skills after two years of college. While some in this group may have learned about their subjects, or matured or benefitted from college in other ways, in these important measures they had no improvement whatsoever. If this study is representative of the college population as a whole, then nearly half of all college students have no gains in any of these vitally important skills after two years of college!

This cohort of students was tested again at college graduation, and results were not much better. As measured by the CLA, 36 percent failed to improve their skills between entering college and graduating four years later. Why is this happening? How could more than one-third of students go through four years of college and not improve in any of these measures? The authors of the study suggest that a lack of rigor is the problem, with few students taking a course that required them to read more than forty pages a week or write more than twenty pages at any point during the semester. Students who did have classes with extensive reading and writing assignments were among those who did improve. Another factor was the lack of time studying outside class. They found that students spent only twelve to fifteen hours per week preparing, and much of that was group study, which has been shown to be less effective

The authors revisited the study cohort a few years after graduation and had responses from almost one thousand of them. It turns out that those with low scores on the CLA, showing no improvement in skills during their college years, were more likely to be unemployed or underemployed than those scoring at the top. Those scoring higher on the CLA were less likely to experience job loss and unemployment, and they were more likely to be financially independent and less likely to be living with their parents.[51]

Is it time to return to a focus on academics in college? The answer is a resounding yes. The American college is changing rapidly, and commonly held views of the future of college life lean toward a more academic nature.

HOW CAN STUDENTS AVOID THE PITFALLS OF COLLEGE LIFE?

You can't underestimate the importance of having a plan for college. Before starting this expensive and crucial time of life, it's important for students to go over each potential danger and consider how they might handle it. Every student should decide how much he or she is going to study, work, and play and then stick to this schedule. The plan is an essential part of building a Success Profile, which is the key to getting the most out of college.

Part Two of this book discusses the Success Profile, and steps to develop it, in detail. Young adults who focus on their Success Profile take charge of their education and their future by accruing the skills, practices, and accomplishments that will take them far in life. Parents can empower their children by encouraging them to focus on elements of the Success Profile.

To ensure that you get the greatest value out of your college experience, you can begin to develop your personal Success Profile during high school and continue throughout college and beyond. Everyone's Success Profile is different, but building one will help any student avoid pitfalls and find academic, leadership, and employment distinction in the future.

STUDENT SUCCESS COURSES

We shouldn't assume that all young adults instinctively know how to succeed at college, either academically or socially. Many colleges offer "Student Success" programs, which are beneficial to young adults as they adjust to campus life. These classes help students to identify campus resources, build study skills, manage their time, and establish relationships with peers and faculty.

For example, in 1979, Boston College started a Learning to Learn program, which is designed to improve students' critical-thinking abilities and help them develop the skills and relationships that they need to excel at college. Learning to Learn is now a federally funded program, adopted by more than one hundred colleges. Other schools, such as Rollins College in Winter Park, Florida, have an Office of Student Success, which helps students thrive academically and navigate the transition to college life. In addition to seminars and programs, these offices have counselors available for one-on-one meetings in which they discuss personal vision statements, four-year plans, and majors.

WHY BOTHER GOING TO COLLEGE AT ALL?

There are people who conclude that college is not worth the price or the bother. They cite dated curriculums useless to current work environments, expensive tuition, and academic "adriftness" and cap it off with stories of technology billionaires and others who succeeded with no college degree.

But the truth of the matter is that, unequivocally, it pays

to go to college. College graduates are doing better than those without degrees in just about every measure of happiness, well-being, and financial success. A study by the Federal Reserve Bank of San Francisco found that the average college graduate made over $800,000 more in his lifetime than a non–college graduate did, and this is after the cost of tuition and lost wages for four years.[52] Bureau of Labor Statistics reports from 2014 show workers with bachelor's degrees earning 40 percent more each week.[53] The degree-holders also benefit from a 2.9 percent unemployment rate, versus a 5.3 percent unemployment rate for those with only a high school diploma.[54]

A recent Pew Research Center study found that millennials with college degrees are outperforming their less-educated peers on nearly every economic measure, and the gap between the two groups has only grown over time. The report found that young adults who have graduated from college had greater job satisfaction, better employment prospects, and a lower likelihood of living at home with their parents. They are also less likely to be living in poverty and more likely to be married.[55] This chart shows why college is worth even more today than it was in the past.

MEDIAN ANNUAL EARNINGS AMONG FULL-TIME WORKERS AGES 25 TO 32, IN 2012 DOLLARS

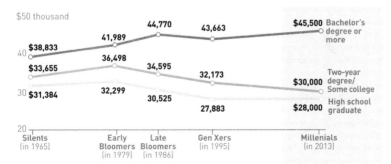

Source: Pew Research Center tabulations of the 2013, 1995, 1986, 1979, and 1965 March Current Population Survey (CPS) IPUMS

PEW RESEARCH CENTER

If you are an ambitious would-be entrepreneur, and you want to model yourself after the leaders in technology who bypassed college and went straight to stardom, think again. These innovators were leaders in their generation and very rare. They did not start a trend of skipping college; they were outliers who simply didn't need it.

However, creative young adults intrigued with skipping college should consider the Thiel Fellowship. Founded by Peter Thiel, an entrepreneur and venture capitalist who has been involved with many of Silicon Valley's most exciting companies, the Thiel Fellowship funds selected young adults under age twenty to skip college and start work on their creative projects. The fellowship's website, www.thielfoundation.org, gives details on how to apply, as well as this description:

> The Thiel Fellowship brings together some of the world's most creative and motivated young people, and helps them bring their most ambitious ideas and projects to life. Thiel Fellows are given a no-strings-attached grant of $100,000 to skip college and focus on their work, their research, and their self-education. They are mentored by our network of visionary thinkers, investors, scientists, and entrepreneurs, who provide guidance and business connections that can't be replicated in any classroom. Rather than just studying, you're doing.[56]

THE SUCCESS

PROFILE—WHAT IT

IS, AND HOW

TO DEVELOP IT

What Is the Success Profile?

In my role as an educational consultant, I have worked one-on-one with students from all over the world, and I've had the benefit of learning from each one of them. I saw teens who were forced into my office by their well-meaning parents, others who were willing to play the college admissions game but were growing weary of it, and some who showed me their authentic selves. The latter group, students who show their authentic selves, do not always have the best grades or SAT scores, but they are usually happy and accomplished. Once, it was the guy who wrote songs on his guitar at home and dreamed of becoming a professional musician, and another time it was a girl who loved children and teaching them and had worked at camps, volunteered at Sunday school, and babysat. These students' light shone through, and I could see that they were living with an authentic sense of purpose.

It turns out that admissions officers also yearn for authenticity; it has become a buzzword in certain circles. Those of us who work with young people can identify authenticity pretty quickly. I have been truly awed by certain students who have crossed my path. It is amazing to talk with an eighteen-year-old with intellectual energy who is curious, ambitious, and impressive in the way he speaks and communicates. He has a vision and enthusiasm for his future and the future of the world. These students are the inspiration behind the Success Profile.

While many factors, including luck, can contribute to success in life, the mainstay seems to be personal qualities. Those personal qualities that tend to lead people to great achievement are what I call the "Success Profile." The Success Profile is slightly different for everyone, but it often involves some combination of the following attributes:

- Grit (commitment/ persistence)
- Curiosity
- Purpose
- A "growth mindset"
- Achievement orientation
- Intellectual passion
- Collaborative attitude
- Ambition
- Self-awareness
- Confidence
- Proactive attitude
- Foresight (consideration of and plans for the future)
- Leadership
- Organization
- Written and oral communicative ability
- Collegiality (forming connections with peers, professors, and others)

These qualities are exhibited by young people, even at a very early age. They are characteristics that get the attention of elite admissions committees, but they are also the attributes that launch students to success in college and careers. We have learned that elite colleges don't offer a golden ticket for professional and personal successes, but I assure you that the Success Profile does. The economists Krueger and Dale postulated that students who are admitted to top-tier colleges but don't attend one earn just as much as those who do attend, suggesting that ambition is a major factor in success. We have also seen that colleges don't transform ordinary students into exceptional ones, but rather collect students who already show potential.

So it's clearly time for an overhaul of the way we think about college. It's time to stop focusing on the "name brand" of a college. It's time for students to stop trying to craft themselves into what they think the colleges want them to be, and start looking inward, developing their own talents and interests, building skills, forging ahead on their own paths, and developing their own Success Profile. Students who want to get an "Ivy League"–quality education should develop themselves in high school in order to take full advantage of college opportunities.

ANY STUDENT CAN DEVELOP HIS OR HER SUCCESS PROFILE

The Success Profile includes personal qualities and habits or behaviors that students can work on and improve. When they are able to enhance their abilities in these areas, they are more likely to achieve. It is not correct to say that these qualities are innate or not likely to change. Youth is a period of extraordinary change and development, and teenagers and young adults can learn a lot just from being told about a new way of thinking or behaving.

If developing a Success Profile sounds like a lot of effort, consider this: teenagers today devote a lot of time to SAT and ACT preparation, and parents may contribute hundreds or even thousands of dollars to pay for classes and tutors. We were all somehow convinced that this was the right thing to do. More often than not, the improvement in test scores from all that preparation is slight and doesn't make a meaningful difference in college admissions; plus, we have seen that college selection has little impact on success, anyway.

For example, I worked with two students who both studied for the SAT for about six months and whose parents paid more than two thousand dollars for private tutoring. The first student started with an 1800 (out of 2400), and she and her parents were both proud that she scored a 1920 after tutoring, a meaningful 120-point improvement. However, it didn't change her college list, and the college she ended up attending accepted more than half of applicants with her original score of 1800, meaning that she probably would have been admitted without retaking the test. My second student was a high achiever, already scoring over 700 in each section of the SAT. He devoted himself to tutoring in hopes of getting his score up and earning an acceptance to an Ivy League college. While his score did go up a little bit in each section, he wasn't admitted to any Ivies. He ended up attending an excellent college that would have probably admitted him with his original score.

My point here is that we have convinced teenagers that studying for the SAT is the smart thing to do, something that will improve their futures. If teens refocus that energy on improving their Success Profile, developing qualities and skills that will help them in the future far more than an increased SAT score would, they will be better off (and will probably spend less money getting there). What if we change the norm and have kids prepare themselves for the real world instead of for college admissions?

The Success Profile is not a concept limited to students who hope to attend elite colleges. Every young person has a unique Success Profile, and it is up to him or her to develop it. Teenagers who struggle with academics in the traditional high school setting often thrive and excel when they look for their passion and pursue interests outside school. The Success Profile is about more than just being a good student from nine am to three pm every day; it is about looking inward, finding how you can make a difference, and following through. Any student with the desire to improve himself and have a more fruitful future will make progress by developing his Success Profile.

The reality of college life and the job market is that things are tough. The more skills that you have going in, the better you are likely to do. If you develop yourself in high school, the benefits will come in spades down the road. You'll reap academic and financial rewards, as well as set yourself up for personal satisfaction, because you will be used to setting goals based on your personal interests and enjoying yourself along the way to achieving them. The next two chapters give instructions on how students can develop their Success Profile starting in high school (or in college, for those just picking up this book), and how the Success Profile can be put into action in college. Once a student has developed her Success Profile, she can get the most out of her college experience and be in the best position to start her career.

YOU ARE CAPABLE OF MORE THAN YOU REALIZE

The most important thing I learned from my Chinese clients is that math ability is not a talent or a wonder, but simply something that a student works at. They tell me that parents in China never doubt their child's ability to learn and excel in higher-level math, because they consider math skills to be like a muscle to be exercised. In countries such as the United States, although some do feel this way, more often you find parents (and even teachers) warning their students about how hard math is. As a result, I see students claiming to be "bad" at math or getting frustrated when they can't learn the concepts with a quick review of their notes.

Compare this to the American view of sports. Most American parents feel that their children can play soccer or any sport and do well if only they practice and take it seriously. American parents dedicate much of their free time to standing on the sidelines and supporting and encouraging their children on the field. My Chinese clients who come to the United States for boarding school are often hesitant about sports and reluctant to try out for a team, feeling that they are not talented in this area, and that talent is what is important in high school sports. In both cases, the students who believe that they have the ability to do well through their own effort are the ones who excel, while the students who consider innate talent a prerequisite are the ones who hang back or give up.

Does your child proclaim herself to be bad at science, terrible at writing, or any other poisonous variant on this theme? A good rule is to never label yourself as bad at anything! In fact, don't label yourself as good at something either. While every child has special interests or preferences, it is important to realize that he, like thousands of students in high schools everywhere, can master any subject and succeed in many areas of interest. See "Develop a growth mindset" (page 66) for more on this critical idea.

Developing the Success Profile
in High School

College success doesn't start in college—it starts in high school! By now, with all I've discussed about the importance of students' active investment in their own education, I hope this isn't surprising to you. If you are a parent or counselor, you can encourage your charges to focus less on intensive test prep and school research and more on preparing themselves to succeed in (and after) any college they attend. With the right mix of positive attitude, determination, introspection, and planning, high school students can develop their own Success Profile by taking the following steps, which this chapter will describe in detail:

SUCCESS PROFILE BUILDING, ACT I:

1. Develop a growth mindset.
2. Start on a path toward a sense of purpose.
3. Explore areas of academic interest in depth.
4. Devise and execute a plan to improve your academic performance.

5. Improve writing, critical thinking, and complex problem-solving skills.
6. Make an impact in an area of interest.

Are you at the tail end of high school or already in college? Don't worry—you can start taking these steps at any time. Take a look at the next chapter (page 84), and you'll see that there are many connections between Act I and Act II of building the Success Profile. Having a goal and a plan for college (page 100) and seeking out jobs and internships (page 112) are good ways to start developing a sense of purpose. Developing skills and routines to help you adapt (page 109) goes hand in hand with improving your academic performance. Even if you've already graduated, you can follow most of the advice in these two chapters.

STEP 1: DEVELOP A GROWTH MINDSET.

Have you ever noticed how people describe others who are exceptionally accomplished as talented, lucky, brilliant, strong, or blessed? We almost see them as superheroes, and whether we admire or envy them, we believe that they have something the rest of us don't. This is part of a "fixed mindset," a belief that one's intelligence, personal qualities, and abilities are things that you can't change very much. The opposite view, called the "growth mindset" believes that it is possible and normal to change ("grow") your intelligence and personal qualities through effort. Developing this growth mindset is the first step in developing your Success Profile.

Mindsets are an important, and changeable, part of your personality that have a tremendous effect on how you view yourself and the world, and how you learn. As Dr. Carol S. Dweck, a professor of psychology at Stanford University and the author of *Mindset: The New Psychology of Success*, explains, a person with a growth mindset believes that effort is what ignites ability and turns it into an accomplishment.[57]

Dr. Dweck describes several studies in which students with the fixed mindset got stuck as soon as something became hard, while those with the growth mindset charged forward and excelled, despite similar academic backgrounds and intelligence. She gives an example of a group of pre-med students, some with a fixed mindset and others with a growth mindset, during their first semester of chemistry.

The students started out with the same level of interest in chemistry, but over the course of the semester, things changed. The students with the fixed mindset stayed interested only if they did well right away. "Those who found it difficult," Dweck writes, "showed a big drop in their interest and enjoyment. If it wasn't a testament to their intelligence, they couldn't enjoy it."[58]

Those who lost interest found it harder to study, and one fixed-mindset student said, "I was excited about chemistry before, but now every time I think about it, I get a bad feeling in my stomach."[59]

The students with the growth mindset also found that the chemistry class got more difficult, yet their enjoyment and interest did not wane. One student commented, "It's a lot more difficult than I thought it would be, but it's what I want to do, so that only makes me more determined."[60] For this student, the challenge fed his interest.

Dweck found that the students with the growth mindset approached their studying in a different way and worked to keep themselves motivated and connected to the course material. One student explained, "I looked for themes and underlying principles across lectures. I went over mistakes until I was certain I understood them."[61] Rather than repeating methods over and over again, they looked for new ways to learn the material and connect it to a larger theme. Instead of focusing on memorizing facts for the upcoming test, they studied to learn. These students were ultimately the ones who earned higher grades in the course.

A growth mindset is an essential part of every Success Profile, as it allows us to confront new challenges, both academic and personal, without losing steam. People with the growth mindset achieve results by doing their best, learning, and getting better and better. They find setbacks and disappointments motivating. They take charge of the processes that bring them success, and they adapt study or practice plans to keep their interest and to get better results. Rather than reading and rereading, they find different ways to learn and stay engaged and interested. People with the growth mindset are less likely to feel burned out or stressed, because they don't get their thrill from winning or getting a good grade, but from overcoming the challenge that they undertook.

Changing your mindset is as easy—and as hard—as considering this theory, believing it, and applying it to your life. It is a crucial first step to developing a Success Profile. Students or parents who want more information on the concept of the growth mindset, including specific steps on how to turn a fixed mindset into a growth mindset, are encouraged to read Carol Dweck's book.

STEP 2: START ON A PATH TOWARD A SENSE OF PURPOSE.

Many young people today are big on ambition but have no real plan for how to reach their goals. They are on the teenage treadmill of success, trying to give the teacher what she needs in order to get the grades that will help them get into a good college. The problem is that kids who are on this track often become unhappy and emerge from high school unable to play the game any longer. They might ask for a year off (a gap year), or simply tune out during college and give themselves the break they need.

William Damon, professor of education at Stanford University and the author of *The Path to Purpose: Helping Our Children Find Their Calling in Life*, writes about a group of students who had accomplished so much in high school that they found little in college to engage them, and did not succeed there. Damon writes:

> These brilliant students would not be losing their motivation in college if they brought with them a better understanding of what they wanted to accomplish and why. If, during those early years of strenuous effort and high achievement, they had found purposes that went deeper than grades and awards, they would have hit the ground running when they entered college. They would have then been eager to gain more knowledge and skills in order to help them better accomplish their chosen careers.[62]

Those students floundered, while other young people mastered their academic work and set the world on fire with innovative ideas and enthusiasm. The difference is a sense of purpose. So what exactly is that, and how does one get it?

Damon gives a definition: "Purpose is a stable and generalized intention to accomplish something that is at the same time meaningful to the self and consequential for the world beyond self." [63] Purpose reaches out beyond the self, and can involve accomplishments that may or may not be achievable in one's lifetime. A person's sense of purpose can change and evolve over time, but at the present, it is the answer to the question of why a person strives, why she is doing something and why it matters. Damon adds, "The pursuit of purpose can organize an entire life, imparting not only meaning and exhilaration but also motivation for learning and achievement." [64]

In the example above, the students had grown up with short-term goals, which were just desires that had no long-term significance. They wanted to get good grades, be the best in the class, or perhaps please their parents. A true purpose is an end in itself. Examples of a sense of purpose include wanting to become a doctor and cure disease, help homeless people by changing government policy, create art, build a business, or have a loving family and the ability to support them. In contrast, goals such as getting a good grade, becoming valedictorian, or getting into a top college are short-term and also self-centered. Purpose, by definition, must involve the world beyond oneself. Damon explains that short-term goals are related to purpose, and are essential in helping people keep moving forward. However, on their own they are insufficient.

How can teenagers develop a sense of purpose? By trying to make a difference to someone, no matter how small, and to be useful to others. Parents can encourage their students in this by opening up opportunities for them to make a difference. Volunteer work can certainly help, but so can paid employment. A student who works at a restaurant or a store gains a sense of helping others and being a part of a larger operation. Some young people today participate only in activities designed to better themselves and never have the experience of being useful. Knowing how to contribute and make a difference, even in a local or mundane area, is an early step to being able to make a difference with regard to causes or interests that they are passionate about.

Damon recommends that finding a path to purpose start with observing purposeful people at work and communicating with people outside the family. This leads to two moments of revelation, when the young person realizes that something important in the world can be improved and that he himself can contribute or make a difference in a small way. The young person identifies a personal purpose, then moves on to developing the skills needed for this pursuit and making a long-term commitment to the purpose. Finally, the young person is able to use the skills and personal strengths in other areas of his life, or even to pursue a different purpose. A person's purpose is not necessarily fixed throughout life; it tends to evolve and change with growth and maturity. It's important that young adults work toward some purpose that is significant to them, even if it may change. There are many true "renaissance men" (and women) out there who work toward several purposes simultaneously.

As parents, we hope that our children lead purposeful lives. Young adults who lead lives with purpose have found something meaningful to involve themselves in, have sustained this interest over time, know why they are pursuing their interest, and have taken thoughtful steps to achieve their dreams. *The Path to Purpose* is a good resource for those who want to learn more, and the next chapter includes many suggestions for how to get going.

Grit: an essential part of the success profile

Grit, by definition, is the tendency to sustain interest in and effort toward very long-term goals. We have all heard about winners in the sports and business worlds who show an extraordinary amount of grit. They don't give up, despite any number of failed ventures or pursuits, or being told they are not good enough. But it's not just business titans and sports stars who have grit: artists and other creative types have to work on their craft, and they go through failed auditions and the rejections of their manuscripts, but because they love what they are doing and are determined, they keep moving forward. In fact, grit is an important quality for success in most areas of life, which is why it is an essential part of the Success Profile.

Angela Duckworth is a psychology professor at the University of Pennsylvania and winner of the 2013 MacArthur Genius Award who studies grit. Her recent research found that grit was the best predictor of success.[65] Duckworth developed a scale and a survey that measure a person's grit. As you might expect, many of the questions measuring a person's grit are about responding with resilience when faced with failure or adversity. But half of the questions are about consistency, dedication, and having "focused passions." Duckworth explains, "It means that you choose to do a particular thing in life and choose to give up a lot of other things in order to do it. And you stick with those interests and goals over the long term."[66]

She found that grit had very little to do with talent, and in some cases was inversely related to talent, showing that perhaps people with special talents had less grit than others. However, she clarifies that "the inverse relationship between talent and grit that we've found in some of our studies doesn't mean that all talented people are un-gritty. That's certainly not true. The most successful people in life are both talented and gritty in whatever they've chosen to do. The people who are, for lack of a better word, 'ambitious'—the kids who are not satisfied with an A or even an A+, who have no limit to how much they want to understand, learn, or succeed—those are the people who are both talented and gritty."[67]

Most interesting is Duckworth's belief that grit can be taught. Schools and parents can show children how grit has been important to the success of others, and how mistakes and failures are normal parts of life and working through disappointments is essential to working at your highest level. If grit sounds familiar, it's because it is intrinsic to developing a "growth mindset." Of course, this sentiment has been around for a long time. The quote "If at first you don't succeed, try, try again" was a popular saying in nineteenth-century schoolbooks, suggesting that even two hundred years ago, educators considered the concept of grit to be worth teaching.

STEP 3: EXPLORE AREAS OF ACADEMIC INTEREST IN DEPTH.

It's extremely important to explore areas of intellectual interest on your own terms, through your own means, and at your own pace. I have known students who learned to code, built rockets, designed video games, wrote screenplays, sketched fashion designs, and self-published books. I also knew a student who was fascinated with World War II history and read about it on his own, a young actor who studied great scenes from classic films, and a young man who analyzed and valued technology stocks. These explorations were not done for a grade and were not performed under anyone else's guidance or guidelines. The teens who explored in this way found it exhilarating and built confidence in their abilities.

If your student doesn't have an intellectual interest, then it is time to explore. Listen for clues about topics or causes that interest them. Ask them if there is something that they dream of doing someday. Give them free time, or connect them with a person who shares one of their interests. Many teens are not used to having time where they are unplugged, unscheduled, and free to pursue interests or curiosities. Given the time and encouragement to explore an area of interest, they often come up with really interesting results. (For teen readers, feel free to ask yourself these questions and give yourself these opportunities—you'll need to structure your own time this way in college, so why not start now?)

Many young people have a dream of what they want to do in the future, and it's surprising to see that they have not learned anything about this field beyond a superficial level. It's as if the future is so far away to them that there's no need to explore it and take early steps on the path to getting there.

These dreamers should be encouraged to develop a plan of how to fulfill their dreams, but also to experience a piece of the dream along the way. If a student wants to be a pediatrician, she should understand the path through medical school and residency, including which science classes are recommended. She should talk to a pediatrician she knows, and try to get an internship or a volunteer role working with children. If she wants to be a documentary filmmaker, she should study the craft, get involved with local filmmakers as an intern, write and produce her own documentary, and stay up to date on current events and issues in the world. And finally, she can research successful filmmakers and how they got there. Check out the next chapter for some more ways to explore interests outside high school.

Teens should also try new things and have new experiences. Sometimes it ignites a passion, and other times it slowly shows how they can make a difference, add value, and contribute to society in some small (or large) way. This exploration is also effective in helping students to discover that perhaps a dream isn't for them after all. If that is the case, on to the next adventure.

STEP 4: DEVISE AND EXECUTE A PLAN TO IMPROVE YOUR ACADEMIC PERFORMANCE.

Academic skills are an essential part of the Success Profile. We have seen throughout this book that students who are strong in critical thinking, complex problem-solving, and communication skills go far in life, no matter what type of college they go to. It is important to get the most out of your high school education, but also to look beyond it and focus on building these skills. There are many good study tips out there, but here are a few that can be helpful to teenagers who are trying to improve their academic skills. Whether a student is at the top of his class or struggling, these tips can take him to the next level academically.

Teenagers who study a lot hate to admit this to their peers. This leaves the non-studiers thinking that no one is really studying much, and that the smart kids just "get it" faster. But in reality, it takes time and commitment to be a good student. Developing a Success Profile requires teens to study more than the typical student, and to also study better. Here's how.

Study hours at home.

We live in a world of 24/7 connectedness, and teens today face enormous distractions from text messages, social media, and television. It is difficult to focus and concentrate with so many bursts of stimulus. The simple solution of turning it all off for a set amount of time during study hours can make a difference in the amount of material that you retain, and in how creative you are.

I learned this lesson from my clients who left public school to attend boarding school. Some of them made the change to take advantage of the learning-support programs offered by boarding schools, and others were good students who switched to rigorous boarding schools for the academic challenge and diverse international environment. I was pleased to hear that many of those who had struggled in the past were now doing well, and that those who were top students were still thriving at their competitive prep schools. When I asked the students whether it was the small classes, the teachers, or some other support that led to their success, I was surprised when most of the kids immediately mentioned study hours. At many boarding schools, the structured day includes a two- to three-hour evening study period during which the school internet connection and phone network is shut down, and students are not allowed to use their smartphones or tablets or watch television. Those with assignments that require Internet use can work in the library under the watchful eye of the librarian. With little to do but study, some students find it easier to become engrossed in their schoolwork for that short time. One girl told me that it was like a huge burden had been lifted, and that she enjoyed her two quiet hours immensely.

A WORD ABOUT STUDYING FOR THE SAT

Parents expect a good SAT tutor to work wonders. They have heard about the importance of test preparation, and they want their children to work hard and do their best, with the helpful guidance of a class or tutor. But the reality is that most students have minimal improvement on the SAT even after studying. The National Association for College Admission Counseling completed a study that concluded that test-prep courses improve SAT scores only by about 10 to 20 points on average in mathematics and 5 to 10 points in critical reading. The College Board, which administers the SAT, says that on average, students who take the SAT test twice only increase their scores by about 30 points. That doesn't sound like a meaningful enough gain to justify the typical course cost of over $1,000, plus the hours of class time, practice tests, and study time.

A few years ago, test-prep companies such as Princeton Review and Kaplan promoted their services by saying that the average increase was 100 points, or even 200 points. They voluntarily stopped making those claims after challenges to the validity of these statements. The president of Princeton Review's test-preparation arm, Scott Kirkpatrick, conceded, telling the *Associated Press*, "Score improvement is not our core mission. I don't want us to be a test-prep company. We need to be an education company."[68]

Boarding schools don't have to be the only places with quiet study hours. Students can create their own study hours by putting electronics in a different room and vowing to leave everything off for two hours. It often works best if the student has specific hours, such as seven to nine pm, each night so that friends and family learn that this isn't a good time to contact them.

It can also be helpful for students to keep track of their actual study time. It's good to take frequent breaks and stay fresh, but to count the number of minutes during which they are actually focusing and studying. The goal is to try to get better each week, with more hours of focused study.

Study each subject differently.

Top students in English and history know that reading and rereading count for a lot, as do writing outlines, identifying themes, and predicting which questions will be asked on a test. When you try to apply this method to math, it often comes up short. Rather than reviewing notes and reading the textbook, top math students know the importance of working through problems and reviewing errors. Math usually needs to be learned by doing, so students who aren't getting the concept through their notes should do more and more problems until they are getting most of them correct.

Study methods can be adapted for different subjects, and successful students keep trying various methods of study and review until they find the ones that work best for them in a particular subject.

Be engaged in class.

Remember that the teacher is not an entertainer at the front of the room whose job is to keep you from drifting off. As an active listener, you should be nodding, watching her, taking notes, and asking questions. Many successful students preview the next day's material during their homework time, so that they have a basic understanding of the material being covered before the teacher presents it.

Get one-on-one help when it's needed.

Personalized tutoring can be a great way to get past a difficult concept or to better understand the material in a difficult class. The teacher is often a good source for extra help (and this is good practice for building relationships with professors once in college—see page 108), as are students in the class who seem to know the material well. A private tutor is an expensive but often helpful option. Students can also turn to online review sites such as Khan Academy (see page 206) for a different approach to the subject.

Develop a study plan for the week.

A successful study plan includes prioritizing preparation for tests, quizzes, and papers, but also time to review the material taught in each class and preview what will be taught the next day.

STEP 5: IMPROVE WRITING, CRITICAL THINKING, AND COMPLEX PROBLEM-SOLVING SKILLS.

Students with developed Success Profiles are strong writers, thinkers, and communicators. All high schoolers should work to enhance these aspects of their personal profiles.

Writing

Words are powerful. People who are effective at using written and spoken language to express their views, support a

point, or analyze a problem are clearly ahead of those who do not have this skill. Good writers are able to organize their ideas and articulate them clearly. Writing is not only about proper grammar or conveying your thoughts clearly; students who write frequently also develop their critical-thinking and critical-reasoning skills, which are crucial in today's job market.

Unfortunately, writing is no longer emphasized at most American high schools. It is pushed aside by curriculums that focus on getting good results on standardized tests or covering extensive amounts of material, which leaves little time for careful analysis and writing. Teachers have large classes and less time to grade writing exercises. They aren't likely to give extensive feedback and edits or encourage students to rewrite. There are very few high school graduates who have written a ten-page research paper, which was a common requirement in past years. Some graduates report writing only a few two- to three-page papers each year. Students who write serious nonfiction know how to tell a story using facts and details from other sources, and they are able to make unique points and support their arguments. This is becoming a rare skill for high school students.

If writing is so important, yet most schools do not have daily writing assignments, what can a student do? Don't rely on your school to turn you into a writer. Write in a journal every day. Write a response to an article that you've read. Write a persuasive essay explaining your point of view. Once you start writing, it might become a habit that stays with you for life.

WRITING RESOURCES FOR STUDENTS

Teen Ink (www.teenink.com) is a website dedicated to teen writing.

The Foundation for Critical Thinking (www.critical thinking.org) offers tutorials called "How to Study and Learn," "The Art of Close Reading," and "Become a Critic of Your Thinking."

Young Writers Society (www.youngwriterssociety. com) is an online forum where you can submit your writing, get tips, and read your peers' writing.

Figment (www.figment.com) is a website connecting writers and readers of all ages.

The Claremont Review (www.theclaremontreview.ca) is an international magazine for young writers

Submit your writing to *Merlyn's Pen* (www.merlyns pen.org) for publication.

Gotham Writers' Workshop has online classes for teen writers at www.writingclasses.com/Course DescriptionPages/Teen.php/ClassTypeCode/T.

When you have honed your craft, consider entering one of the hundreds of writing contests in Appendix 2.

Critical thinking and complex problem-solving

Many students don't know what exactly critical thinking is, much less how to improve it. In fact, the *Wall Street Journal* ran an October 2014 article titled "Bosses Seek Critical Thinking, but What Is That?"[69] The article noted the frequent use of the term "critical thinking" in job postings and from hiring firms, but also noted that there seemed to be many understandings of its meaning. The *Oxford English Dictionary*'s simple definition is "objective analysis and evaluation of an issue in order to form a judgment." But critical thinking goes beyond that and includes the ability to engage in reflective and independent thinking. It also goes hand-in-hand with problem-solving skills.

Dr. Joe Lan and Dr. Jonathan Chan from the University of Hong Kong philosophy department describe a strong critical thinker as someone who can understand the logical connections between ideas, construct arguments, detect common mistakes in reasoning, solve problems systematically, and identify the importance of ideas. They write, "A critical thinker is able to deduce consequences from what he knows, and he knows how to make use of information to solve problems, and to seek relevant sources of information to inform himself."[70]

Now that we know what critical thinking is, how does a student get better at it? Some professors advise a study of the laws of logic and methods of scientific reasoning. Students might benefit from learning about the logical structure of an argument, and then trying to apply that to a simple problem. Students are encouraged to read, question, think of alternative points of view, and gather evidence to support their view—essentially "Thinking about your thinking, while you're thinking, in order to improve your thinking," as Linda Elder, president of the Foundation for Critical Thinking, advises. Her organization's website has excellent tutorials and exercises to help people of all ages improve their critical-thinking and complex problem-solving skills.

STEP 6: MAKE AN IMPACT IN AN AREA OF INTEREST.

There is something invigorating about starting a big project: the ideas, initial materials, research, enthusiasm, and hope that the project will grow to help or be interesting to others.

Young adults can learn a great deal about themselves and their interests and qualities by trying to achieve in an area of interest. The key is to have a plan for the project and then to follow through, adjusting your plans or expectations as needed. Of course, not every project will produce the planned result, but it's important to pursue it as far as you can.

I know students who started their own businesses in the areas of babysitting, lawn service, and computer tutoring. Some students do volunteer projects; a young musician raised money and collected instruments to send to impoverished schools abroad. Others pursue national and international awards, which are opportunities to compete against students worldwide. Chapter Eight has a complete overview of contests and awards, which are exceptional ways for students to achieve.

ACTION IDEAS FOR SUCCESS

- Develop a global view and get out of your comfort zone: Read five news articles a week from countries other than your own.
- Be tech-savvy: Take an online programming course or an InDesign tutorial.
- Be entrepreneurial: Start your own small business.
- Show initiative: Start a new student organization.
- Become a communicator: Write for ten minutes a day, every day, for at least a month.
- Think beyond yourself: Do something that will impact a person or group of people.
- Be compassionate: Help someone and try to learn about his or her life.
- Be creative: Write, draw, paint, sculpt, photograph, or film something.

WHY THE SUCCESS PROFILE IS EFFECTIVE

The Success Profile empowers students to look inward and develop themselves, realizing that they will determine their own future success. When students step away from the getting-into-college frenzy and focus on things that will truly help them, we typically see increased self-confidence, skills, and future success.

The Success Profile starts with the development of a growth mindset and a sense of purpose, as well as specific personal qualities and work habits. It's important to realize that these practices can be learned. Habits can be improved on and qualities can be developed; they are not innate.

The other elements of the Success Profile are more concrete: teenagers should pursue their intellectual interests in depth, or explore new things. They are tasked with taking their academic program seriously, working hard, and getting good results. They are asked to go above and beyond what their high school offers by developing their skills in complex problem-solving, communication, and critical thinking. And finally, students can achieve by taking on a project and hoping it will have a positive impact on others. Students who have mastered these six elements of the Success Profile are positioned well to take on the challenges of college life.

When High School Isn't Enough: How to Go Above and Beyond in Developing the Success Profile

Who says that the local high school should be the site of all of a student's academic progress? The curriculum doesn't always allow for in-depth analysis of a subject, long research papers, or intensive science projects. But for many students, both those at the top of the class and those who struggle, it is exactly this type of hands-on, experiential work that excites them and helps them to progress academically.

The most interesting academic projects that I have seen or heard about have been completed outside school. Students have done incredible, lasting work for the Intel Science Talent Search; they have published works of writing, won math competitions, built model NASA moon-rover buggies, and written plays that have been produced. Even those who don't enjoy school have found success by becoming immersed in extracurricular projects such as building a robot, giving a speech, or creating art.

Two essential steps in developing the Success Profile involve exploring areas of intellectual interest and trying to achieve in these areas. This chapter offers resources and ideas for students who want to look beyond their high school for intellectual opportunities. This includes information on national and international award programs, online classes and diploma programs, semester and summer programs, and early college.

AWARDS AND OTHER HONORS

It feels fantastic to win an award, no matter what your age, and it is a great way to put Step 6 into practice and make an impact (see page 81). Whether it is a new area that a student discovers, or something she has been passionate about for most of her life, it is an incredible thrill to be challenged and measured against others throughout the world.

Many people know about national rankings for high school sports stars, but some are surprised to know that it isn't only athletes who can compete with students from across the country and the world. There are opportunities for writers, musicians, scientists, activists, artists, web designers, orators, and others to compete nationally, or even internationally. Testing your performance against the best young adults out there can be invigorating and inspiring.

There are hundreds of awards and contests open to high school students. These competitions are not related to grades or in-school performance, so even those who have not been inspired by school may enjoy delving deep into a subject of interest. Below, I have described just a few of them in depth; Appendix 2 has a list of more than two hundred awards and competitions for high school students in everything from volunteerism to robotics to public speaking. It's a great resource for any student who hopes to challenge himself, pursue an interest outside school, and compete with the nation's best.

U.S. Presidential Scholars in the Arts

Many artists dream of performing at the Kennedy Center for the Performing Arts or having their work displayed at the Smithsonian. The twenty students who are named U.S. Presidential Scholars in the Arts each year achieve that before they have even graduated from high school. They also win a monetary prize of up to $10,000, access to master classes with world-renowned artists, inclusion in a prestigious artists' network, and a launching pad to a career in the arts. The Presidential Scholars are named based on their extraordinary artistic, academic, and creative achievement, and on their success in the YoungArts program, which is open to a larger number of students.

YoungArts is a non-profit that invests in the artistic development of talented young visual, literary, design, and performing artists. More than eleven thousand students apply to YoungArts, either through an audition or by submitting a portfolio. The top seven hundred students are selected to participate in YoungArts Week in Miami, or in one of its regional affiliate programs in New York and Los Angeles. The 170 students who attended YoungArts Miami in January 2014 had the opportunity to work with distinguished master teachers and mentors in their fields. Each night these talented young artists impressed audiences with performances, readings, film screenings, and art exhibitions. The U.S. Presidential Scholars in the Arts were selected from among them after judges considered their artistic achievements and academic profiles.

YoungArts alumni can be found working at the highest levels in the arts worldwide. Alumni include actresses Vanessa Williams, Viola Davis, and Kerry Washington; four-time Tony Award nominee Raúl Esparza; American Ballet Theater CEO Rachel Moore; recording artists Nicki Minaj and Chris Young; musicians Terence Blanchard, Eric Owens, and Jennifer Koh; choreographer Desmond Richardson; and internationally acclaimed multimedia artist Doug Aitken.

Concord Review

The Concord Review: A Quarterly Review of Essays by Students of History is the only quarterly journal in the world to publish the academic work of high school students. The journal selects exemplary history essays with an average of 6,000 words that are written by students from forty different countries. The best essays are awarded the Ralph Waldo Emerson Prize. The *Concord Review* has been lauded by historian and writer David McCullough, who wrote, "I very much like and support what you're doing with the *Concord Review*. It's original, important, and greatly needed, now more than ever, with the problem of historic illiteracy growing steadily worse among the high school generation nearly everywhere in the country."

The late historian and author Arthur M. Schlesinger, Jr., said: "The *Concord Review* offers young people a unique incentive to think and write carefully and well . . . [and] inspires and honors historical literacy. It should be in every high school in the land."

The process for most students starts with an in-school assignment for a short paper, which they become immersed in and decide to turn into a longer paper to submit to the *Concord Review*. Some students hear about the program from guidance counselors or friends and start on a project on their own. They often spend a year or more on their papers, reading primary sources, researching, and writing extensively.

Ye Eun Charlotte Chun was an author in the Winter 2011 issue of the *Concord Review*. Despite having started her submission as a paper for an AP English Language and Composition class, Ye Eun stepped beyond the confines of her assignment to explore urbanization policies in South

Korea firsthand. For two years, she visited slums called "vinyl villages" around Seoul, focusing particularly on Hwahweh Maeul, a squatter village near her high school, for which she fund-raised over $12,000 to install water purifiers.

Reflecting on her experience, Ye Eun said that the *Concord Review* had opened doors for her in ways she had never imagined: "What started off as a paper for a class ended up becoming an academic fixation for me. Since my submission, I have studied urbanization policies around the world, visiting cities like Beijing, Paris, and soon to be London to learn about them *in situ*. I have also decided to minor in urban studies, focusing particularly on developmental urbanization policies.

"In high school, I doubt I would have imagined myself publishing so much of my written work, yet here I am publishing almost every month," Ye Eun reflected. In the past year alone, she has written for *BBC News* and *World Policy Journal*, exploring issues like the gender gap and poverty. Ye Eun is now a student at Princeton University, but it was her dedication to an extracurricular academic project that opened doors for her, not her college.

"To be honest, I don't think I will pursue a professional career in journalism. Even so, the *Concord Review* has motivated me to step outside my comfort zone in ways I would never have imagined. I became a scholar, a writer, and a better human being for it."

Congressional Award

If it seems like long odds to win an award, the good news is that there are honors that are nonselective and can be earned by anyone. The Congressional Award is a major youth award given by the United States Congress to thousands of students every year. Students do not win this award; they earn it. It is voluntary, individual, noncompetitive, and open to all young people ages thirteen to twenty-four. Whether a student is academically motivated or challenged, enthusiastic about school or bored with it, the Congressional Award is an option for him or her.

Students embark on a journey of goal-setting and activities in each of four program areas: Volunteer Public Service, Personal Development, Physical Fitness, and Expedition/Exploration. Depending on the number of hours committed, they can earn a Bronze, Silver, or Gold Congressional Award.

Mark Stuart of Jacksonville, Florida, earned the Gold Award. He served more than one hundred hours at a men's homeless shelter for his Voluntary Public Service requirement. For his Personal Development requirement, he studied the guitar, and for Physical Fitness, he trained with his travel soccer team. Mark enjoyed his expedition, which was a three-night canoe and camping trip in the Florida everglades. Kathleen Donnelly of New Jersey earned her Silver Award by volunteering in a nursing home, studying Irish step dancing and Irish harp, and taking a service expedition to New Orleans.

The students each have an advisor who ensures that they meet their goals. While the Congressional Award is not selective, it is a large commitment and a great achievement. Best of all, young people are able to set their own goals and explore subjects and causes outside of school, at their own pace.

ONLINE CLASSES AND DIPLOMA PROGRAMS

In today's connected society, students are not limited by th courses offered at their local high schools. They can regis' for an online class to supplement their school schedul they can enroll full-time in an online high school. I increasingly popular opportunity, and although it isn't for everyone, it's clear that online high schools are here to stay.

Students enroll in the full-time program for the flexibility or the opportunity to attend school in a unique way that is appealing to them. Some want a break from a traditional public school without giving up on academic life, while others may live in a region with poor academic options. Young artists and athletes with busy practice schedules find online high schools to be an ideal way to schedule classes around other commitments. Gracie Gold, a 2014 winter Olympic figure skater, was a student at the University of Missouri Online High School (now known as Mizzou K–12 Online).

More than half of online high school students are not registered full-time and only take one or two classes in addition to their full schedule at their local school. They are eligible to take any course offered by the online high schools, but the most popular options are Advanced Placement classes. Not every high school offers a full array of AP courses, so students who are looking to challenge themselves at this level are happy to find choices outside their schools. Also, some schools have limited availability in AP classes and do not allow all interested students to enroll. The online high schools are more open and willing to give a chance to these students.

The more-established online high schools are Stanford University Online High School, George Washington University High School, the University of Miami Global Academy, Mizzou K–12 Online, BYU Independent Study Program, and University of Texas High School. The price of an individual course ranges from $195 at UT to $3,640 at Stanford.

In September 2014, edX launched a high school initiative, offering twenty-six Massive Open Online Courses (MOOCs) specifically to this age group (see page 193 for more on MOOCs). They offer AP courses as well as introductory classes in algebra, geometry, psychology, and other subjects. These courses can supplement a student's course in her own high school, or they can be taken independently to explore new areas of interest. The high school courses were developed by UC Berkeley, MIT, Davidson, Georgetown, Rice, and other institutions. EdX courses are free and open to students throughout the world.

The Stanford OLHS is a unique and forward-thinking program that is sure to grow in size and prestige over the next few years. Imagine going to a high school with students from forty-two of the fifty United States and twenty-one countries, learning from one another and from accomplished teachers, 66 percent of whom hold PhD degrees. Stanford OLHS was founded in 2006 with a mission to provide a challenging education to gifted students who are intellectual risk-takers. The school approach focuses on advanced academic offerings and the development of critical thinking and argumentation, intellectual maturity, and responsibility. The program offers typical high school classes, but also twenty-three "post-AP" classes, or early-college-level classes, with titles such as "The Hero and His Opponents in the Classical World" and "Models of Writing and Argumentation."

The Stanford OLHS classes are fully interactive, and students learn as much from one another as they do from the professor. Classes have about fifteen students who all log in at the appointed time, whether they are in the United States, Asia, or anywhere else in the world. They all watch a live-streamed lecture, which uses video clips, whiteboard drawings, and other animations. When students have a question or comment, they click into a queue. When teachers call on them, the rest of the class can see that student from his webcam and hear his question. Stanford OLHS also has an instant-message function that allows for constant discussion for the students as they participate in the class. Claire Goldsmith, the director of External Relations and Admissions at OLHS, said, "Our discussion seminars are highly interactive and totally discussion-based, so students must participate in class and come on camera, and the camera always follows the speaker. We are a 'flipped' classroom in that much of the reading, writing, labs, watching lectures, etc., happens asynchronously outside of class, and the synchronous class time is meant to be engaging and interactive."

Full-time students at Stanford OLHS have a vibrant student life, with online clubs and activities, homeroom, and assembly; an in-person graduation weekend; and an in-person two-week summer program. Students also get together on a regular basis with others who live near them. There are many ways in which students see one another outside of classtime and in which instructors and advisors work closely with students. This unique model for high school education is recognized by colleges and enjoyed by students who love an academic challenge and an innovative way to attend high school.

Whether a student ventures outside his home school to take only one class online or enrolls full-time in an online high school, he is likely to find a unique and valuable experience. It's encouraging to know that students can pursue challenges, or take their academics to the next level, without the limitations of what is offered locally.

SEMESTER AND SUMMER PROGRAMS

Colleges open their doors wider in the summer and offer all sorts of academic and extracurricular residential programs. Some are only a week long and nonselective, while others require an application, involve six to eight weeks of study, and offer college credit upon completion. Summer can be a great time to take classes that aren't offered in a typical high school or get a taste of living in a college dorm. These programs offer some financial aid, but they still tend to be expensive: $8,000 for the Harvard Summer School Secondary School Program, or $6,100 for a four-week residential course at Brown University. Appendix 2 lists a small number of free summer programs.

Adventurous young adults can leave their high school for a semester to attend a "semester school," where they continue academic coursework while focusing on experiential learning. Students interested in environmental studies can attend Conserve School in Wisconsin; those who want to learn to be thoughtful leaders can attend the School for Ethics and Global Leadership in Washington, DC, and those interested in an immersion in island life can head to the Bahamas for the Island School. City Term uses New York City as its classroom and laboratory, while the Mountain School brings teenagers to a working farm in Vermont, and the Ocean Classroom uses a schooner and a three-thousand-mile ocean voyage as its setting. Teenagers who are passionate about visual arts spend a semester at the Oxbow School in Napa, California, while those who want to make a difference in the world head to the Woolman Semester in Nevada City, California, to study and practice peace, social justice, and sustainable living.

The semester-school programs deliver powerful outcomes for students at a crucial juncture in their education. These students reflect on themselves as learners and get the benefits of participating in a small community and being a valuable part of that group. The semester-school programs are a complement to a high school curriculum, a way to go above and beyond and explore an area in depth in a residential community. More information on these and several other programs can be found at www.semesterschool.net. Like the summer school programs, the semester experiences are quite expensive, costing about half the cost of a year at a residential boarding school. Financial aid is available, and some semester programs report as many as 30 percent of their students receiving aid, although these are typically partial scholarships.

ERIC S. CHEN, SCIENCE CONTEST WINNER

Imagine coming close to finding a cure for the flu while you are still in high school. Eric S. Chen of San Diego first became interested in influenza in 2009, when there was an outbreak of the deadly H1N1, or "swine flu." He researched on his own, and then spent several years working in labs with two mentors who were professors at UC San Diego.

Eric hoped to have his work recognized by entering several of the ultra-competitive national science fairs: the Intel Science Talent Search (founded as the Westinghouse Science Talent Search) has a prestigious 72-year history; it has seen seven participants win Nobel Prizes and eleven win MacArthur Foundation "Genius" grants. The world-renowned Siemens Westinghouse Competition in Math, Science, and Technology was founded in 1999, and the newcomer Google Science Fair was inaugurated about ten years later. Eric won all three of these competitions during his senior year.

Eric's project sought an effective medication that could save lives during flu outbreaks. He used computer modeling to identify compounds that were potential flu inhibitors, then tested the inhibitors in a lab. He had positive results, finding several inhibitors that have the potential to be developed into flu medications.

Eric has a patent on his research and hopes that his results will help save lives someday. Eric has a great sense of purpose in his life and was not driven only by the potential of winning the science-fair prize (a short-term goal). By achieving in his area of interest, he also intends to help others throughout the world. He is hopeful that his findings will someday lead to a major medical breakthrough for influenza.

DUAL ENROLLMENT

People are often surprised at how easy it can be for a high school student to get a taste of college. In "dual enrollment," students are enrolled at both a high school and a college. Some students take community college courses and work toward an associate's degree, and others take classes at local state or private universities.

Ankit Gandhi of Tampa, Florida, took sixteen classes at the University of South Florida while he was still a high school student. He did it in part to challenge himself and partly because he thought it would help him when he entered higher education. Ankit was admitted to many top colleges, including Duke and MIT, but he decided to attend Penn State and its Accelerated Pre-Medical/Medical School Program. His credits allowed him to enter college as a junior and put him on a faster track to his career in medicine.[71]

College courses are a great way to get a new academic experience and pursue a subject of interest. The credits may or may not be helpful to your degree progression in the future, depending on the college program and major you choose. The best reasons to take a college class are to challenge yourself, build your academic skills, and explore an area of interest.

INDEPENDENT RESEARCH

Many young people become very good at high school without becoming curious or interested learners. Anything the teacher gives them will be worked on and returned, with no extra thought or research. It's a very different process from that of an intellectually curious student who seeks alternative ways to learn about a subject of interest.

This chapter mentions award programs, online classes, summer or semester programs, and college classes as means of going above and beyond what is offered at a typical high school. But students can also challenge themselves though their own research and projects. Independent exploration builds a great many areas of the Success Profile: it helps you set out on a path to purpose (see page 68), it sets you up to make an impact (see page 81), and it's a good way to improve your study habits (see page 74), because it requires you to organize your own time and motivate yourself.

Eric Chen (profiled opposite) was working on his influenza research for many years before he entered and won contests, and many *Concord Review* writers (see page 87) spent more than a year perfecting their crafts. They found a sense of purpose in their projects, and their interest went far beyond the high school level. Even if you aren't going to win a national award for your work, it's important to explore areas of interest beyond the limited high school curriculum. This can be one of the simplest and most affordable ways to go beyond high school, since all you need is access to the Internet, a library, and possibly a lab.

Developing the Success Profile in College

The hard-fought academic race is not over when the acceptance letter from a college arrives. Although it may feel like a victory, a new set of challenges is on the horizon. As we've seen in past chapters, the college experience has many potential pitfalls (see page 53), as well as the opportunity for great achievement and understanding. It's important to develop a plan for academic success and personal happiness at college.

Those lucky few whose acceptance letters were from elite colleges should not assume that their ticket has been stamped and they can coast through college. They will have to compete with talented and hungry young adults from across the country for limited jobs in their fields. They may be job-hunting many years in the future, when it's likely that employers will pay increasingly less attention to the name brand of the college attended and more attention to a candidate's skill set and professional achievements. Most students who are admitted to elite colleges have already developed many attributes of the Success Profile during high school. If they want to remain competitive in the job market, it's important to continue to develop skills and interests, and to carry out Act II of developing their Success Profile.

Students who are going to less-selective colleges should know that their future is in their own hands, and their success will not be determined by the college they attend. They can examine what it is that makes elite students do so well and adopt some of their practices for themselves. Every student can develop his or her own Success Profile, building on personal qualities and achievements that will lead to academic and professional distinction in the future.

The concept of the Success Profile reframes the discussion about college admissions, goals, and success. It asks students to take charge of their own education and future. It asks parents to take the lead in recognizing the hype of the admissions process, and in empowering their students to complete Act I of their Success Profile development before they get to college, then focus on Act II during their college years. (However, if you're just picking this book up and college is already in session, you can work on both acts simultaneously.)

When I asked one of my graduating senior clients about her goals for college, she responded, "I'm going to make new friends, maybe join the crew team, and I'm going to be sure not to take any hard classes in my first semester since I'll be adjusting to college life." Unfortunately, this preference for easy classes often continues well past the first semester and can cheat a student out of an academic experience that will help her develop her skills for the future. College is a time for students to connect with other students and professors, have new experiences, and stretch academically. It's not advised to start with a focus on easy classes.

College is about more than just grades, and developing the Success Profile therefore involves achieving beyond the walls of your college classrooms. This may sound familiar from Act I of Success Profile development (page 65). While it's recommended to start working on one's Success Profile during high school, this is an ongoing journey that's never really completed. Therefore, college students and young adults can continue to build upon their Success Profile, Act I, and evaluate how it is playing a role in their lives during college. But in order to develop a Success Profile for long-term success, students have to grapple with the college-specific goals of Act II. These are research-proven initiatives that will help students to emerge from college ready for the next stage of their lives.

DEVELOPING THE SUCCESS PROFILE, ACT II

1. Do not take on more than a reasonable amount of student loan debt.
2. Have a goal and a plan for college.
3. Get an "Ivy League" education at whatever college you attend.
4. Develop skills and routines that help you adapt and excel in college.
5. Focus on paid employment and internships.
6. Develop communication skills, both spoken and written.
7. Work in a team. If possible, lead a team.
8. Step out of your comfort zone.

STEP 1: DO NOT TAKE ON MORE THAN A REASONABLE AMOUNT OF STUDENT LOAN DEBT.

Many young people today are crippled by student loans. If a parent takes just one thing from this book, I hope that she will realize that she does not have to overextend for college or encourage her child to do so. Students developing their Success Profile can't be saddled by extensive debt, since it has been proven to inhibit their ability to move forward in their adult lives.[72]

Student-loan debt itself is not a bad thing. Loans are what make college a possibility for most Americans, and many success stories would not have been written without student loans. It's *too much* debt that is a bad thing. Before taking out a loan, students should consider a reasonable estimate of their future salary, total debt levels, and potential monthly budget after college. There are always money-saving options to evaluate. A student can attend a state university rather than a private college, or apply to private universities that are likely to offer merit aid. Those who find flagship state universities too expensive can attend a cheaper, regional state university or community college for the first two years. Accelerated degree programs can save money, as can a year of study abroad (see page 118). Each student should evaluate options and chose the debt level that works for him.

Lower-income families should keep in mind that private institutions with large endowments may be able to provide grants (which do not need to be paid back) that cover much or even all of the costs to attend. It is very difficult to predict the actual costs of education until you have been accepted and received your financial aid package. At that point, you should compare the real costs to attend each school that you've been accepted to and make sound financial decisions as a family. Try to avoid letting "sticker shock" keep you from applying in the first place.

For in-depth information on financial decision-making, see page 156.

STEP 2: HAVE A GOAL AND A PLAN FOR COLLEGE.

College is uncharted territory for teenagers. They may be moving far away from home, living independently for the first time, and finding themselves with a daily schedule that is very different from their high school routine. The academic program is different from what they were used to in high school, with fewer assessments along the way (so each essay and test counts for more). Students who are also working, playing a varsity sport, and/or pledging a fraternity or sorority are experiencing an additional set of new challenges. All of these new routines and experiences can be a big blur unless structure and goals are added. Unfortunately, more often than not, students do not set any goals for themselves or think about the obstacles that they may encounter. They typically embark on their new lives with hopes for happiness and success, yet no formal plan of how to get there.

Many top students set goals for themselves before they even get to college. Ideally, goals should be written down, referred to every day, and possibly shared with a friend or family member. Goals should be as specific as possible, and students should brainstorm specific supporting actions that will help them meet the goal. There should also be notes on potential obstacles, strategies to overcome them, and adjustments to the plan if and when necessary.

Ethan, a student at Michigan State University, said, "My goal was to get all As and Bs in my first semester. My plan to support this was to visit each professor at least once, and study every Sunday through Thursday. Potential obstacles were procrastination and fun things coming up that could distract me." Ethan's plan worked well through midterms, and then he needed to make an adjustment. "I realized that meeting with the professors was so helpful that I started to go to each professor about every other week or so with my questions and thoughts. Also, there was too much going on during the week to limit my study times to Sunday through Thursday. I needed to map out each week and set a schedule with study hours spread out over all seven days. I ended up getting straight As, so I surpassed my goal!"

Jackie, a Georgetown University junior planning to enter politics, said, "I had three main goals for college: I wanted to take at least a few of the classes taught by well-known politicians or diplomats. I wanted to get first-hand experience on the Hill through an internship, and I wanted to be sure my grades were high enough that I'd have a better chance at a good job down the road."

Goals and plans are an essential part of developing the Success Profile. We know from research that goals can drive positive behaviors and boost performance in college. Students who are at risk for depression are especially likely to benefit from a structured schedule, as are those who tend to procrastinate. But all students who want to have a better chance of success at college will find that setting goals, making a plan, and developing a schedule will increase their chances of getting there.

STEP 3: GET AN "IVY LEAGUE" EDUCATION AT WHATEVER COLLEGE YOU ATTEND.

We saw in previous chapters that Ivy League universities do not have a monopoly on quality education or on superior outcomes and futures. This chapter is all about getting an "Ivy League" education at whatever college you attend, and this section contains advice on some of the best possible ways to do it. When I use the term "Ivy League" here, I am referring not to the specific colleges in the Ivy League athletic conference, but to the American dream of an excellent college education and experience that can propel a child from one social class to another, helping her reach her goals and have a bright future. I suggest that elite colleges do not transform people in this way or offer opportunities that are much greater than those offered by a regular college. It is the student, not the college, who determines future success. An

"Ivy League" education doesn't happen by osmosis. You can't just show up, fulfill basic requirements, and get a better education than you would at a less-prestigious college. However, students who seek out "Ivy League" value at their own colleges may end up getting superior educational experiences by making specific decisions and choices along the way.

How can you get "Ivy League" value at any college? The steps for building the Success Profile are designed to ensure that students get the most value out of their educations. Every point in the plan is geared toward helping young people get an "Ivy League" experience at whatever college they attend. Successful students take more classes with extensive reading and writing requirements, study more, meet with professors more often, and get more involved with on-campus organizations and activities. It is possible to examine what it is that successful people do during their college years and replicate it. Here's how.

The importance of course selection

It's tempting to register for classes that require very little preparation and whose teachers are known for giving easy As. But those easy classes aren't of much value and should be avoided. Here are six course-selection suggestions that will help students to get the most value out of their college years.

1. Take several classes with heavy reading and writing requirements. Many students never take an English class beyond their Freshman Composition requirement and miss out on the opportunity to develop higher-order thinking skills by participating in classes that frequently require them to produce cohesive arguments. As we'll discuss in Chapter 8 (page 120), employers want to hire individuals who can write well, synthesize ideas, and clearly formulate their opinions, so it is important to develop these skills in college. Arum and Roksa's study found that classes with extensive reading and writing requirements increase improvement in students' skills during the first two years of college. Writing or reading alone did not have the impact that courses heavy in both areas did.

Andrew Roberts, assistant professor of political science at Northwestern University and author of *The Thinking Student's Guide to College*, adds that nearly as important as the quantity of writing during college is the feedback: "You need to hand in the assignment, get critical comments, and incorporate these comments into future assignments or even revisions of the same piece." He further advises that students benefit most from classes that require frequent short papers, since the intense writing with feedback engages the student, fosters a connection with the professor, and improves the students' understanding of the material.[73]

2. Take small seminar classes when possible. They promote active learning, discussion, and engaging with classmates and professors, which is a more beneficial experience than a passive lecture class. Roberts comments on the way that seminars require students to fully engage with the course material: "Because you are in the spotlight during every class and forced to put forward your own ideas, you will have to actively digest your assignments. Not only will you be under pressure to do the reading—something that slips by the wayside in large lecture courses—but you have to think about it and come up with insights and criticisms to share in class."[74] Another added benefit of the seminar-style course is that it allows students to get to know a professor on more than a superficial level. Students are advised to keep their eyes open for seminar classes at course-registration time.

3. Register for classes given by the top professors at your college. The quality and expertise of the professor are very important. This does not necessarily mean that a student should consult Rate My Professors or any other student evaluation website, since those ratings are often based on whether the professor is entertaining and an easy grader. Students can ask for course recommendations from professors and from other serious students at their colleges. Roberts notes in his book that students can evaluate professors' classroom performance by considering a few important points. He writes that good professors give students the opportunity to participate in class, base their lectures around a problem or puzzle, and ultimately show students the relevance of the material they are covering.[75] When registering for lecture-based courses, try to determine whether the professor fits this description.

4. Take courses that build on one another or align with other courses. This gives you a chance to study an area in depth, or to see a subject matter from more than one perspective. An example could be to take a class on urban planning while also taking a sociology class that examines problems in inner-city communities. It's also important to build on classes you have already taken by enrolling in more-advanced classes in the same subject. Some students use up many of their electives taking introductory classes, and while this type of exploration might be interesting, it doesn't go very deep into the topic. Students considering graduate schools should be sure they are taking the courses required for their intended program.

5. Place greater value on content and quality than on the time, location, or convenience of the class. Students are tempted to avoid early-morning classes or give themselves Fridays off, but these logistical decisions shouldn't be primary in building a course schedule.

6. Major in a subject that you love. Many people disagree with this statement, and they will point to evidence that majors such as engineering or business offer training that is more likely to lead to a job, and usually a job with a higher salary. However, I believe that if a student has found a subject that he loves and enjoys, it will be reflected in his grades, his appetite for learning and intellectual curiosity, and his confidence in himself, which will likely lead to career opportunities. The person who slogged away in mechanical engineering out of a sense of duty may not have the grades or knowledge to be successful in that field anyway.

The undergraduate major is not directly connected to career options in the way that many people think it is. A recent *Career Builder* poll found that only half of recent graduates were working in the field related to what they studied in college.[76] I know several people who were psychology majors in college. Their careers almost twenty years out of college are interesting and varied. One did go on to earn a PhD in psychology and is working as a neuropsychologist at a medical practice. But the others include an investment banker, a hedge fund marketer, an IBM consultant, two lawyers, a second-grade teacher, and a public relations director for a major concert venue. There are many examples of people who majored in a subject they enjoyed and were able to do well in, then went on to a career that was ostensibly unrelated. While it is true that some fields, such as medicine and engineering, require a specific degree program, there are many career paths that are flexible regarding the college major.

Students can get a better education for themselves by choosing the right classes. A student who choses many large lecture classes, those known to have few reading or writing requirements and few opportunities for discussion, with less skilled professors, is not going to get the same value as a student who carefully selects small seminars, top professors, and frequent reading and writing, with a cohesive plan of courses that build upon one another.

Study a lot and study alone.

It is common sense and stating the obvious to advise that studying more will produce better results. Indeed, a student who has already completed Act I of developing her Success Profile will have already begun studying more, and more efficiently, in high school. Yet some college students don't know how many hours each week they are devoting to study, nor do they know how many hours a week they should be studying. As we discussed on page 49, a typical course load is fifteen weekly hours of classes, and there should be two hours of preparation time for every hour in class. The result is thirty hours of study time and fifteen hours in class, making a full-time week of forty-five hours. However, this is very rare in real life; most students don't even spend fifteen hours studying. Arum and Roksa found that college students, on average, study only twelve hours a week, with 37 percent of students admitting to studying less than five hours each week.[77] They also noted that students at selective colleges studied about three hours more per week than students at regular colleges. Students developing their Success Profile and trying to get the most value out of their college experience should *at least* match what the students at selective colleges are doing, which is studying seventeen hours per week, and ideally they should aim for thirty. Students can add study time to their weekly schedules or set a timer to see how much they are really studying.

Those who are tempted to add the hours spent in the library with friends as study time should think again. The Arum and Roksa study found that "All hours spent studying are thus not the same: studying alone is beneficial, but studying with peers is not."[78] They found that the more of a student's study time was spent alone, the better he did on the CLA test, and the more of a student's studying was done with peers, the smaller the improvement on the CLA. It leads us to question whether group study is really beneficial at all. Some students say that study groups work well only after they have studied the material extensively alone, and then they are able to bring their questions to the group.

Interact with faculty.

A common worry of students applying to graduate school is how they will get a recommendation from a professor for the application, when they graduated without getting to know any professors well. Professors admit to getting many requests from students who they don't know or remember. The Gallup-Purdue study on links between college, work, and well-being showed that one of the great benefits of college is having a faculty mentor or discussing issues of interest with a professor,[79] but it seems that too few students are taking advantage of this opportunity.

The benefits are not only for those who are in need of graduate school recommendations. Students who meet with a professor to discuss material in class report better understanding, new insights, and stronger grades. Those who get to know a professor well enough to discuss career options or the world outside the class benefit from having an interested, non-relative adult in their lives. Gallup-Purdue found that adults were 2.2 times more likely to report being engaged at work if they had a mentor at college who encouraged them.[80]

The best way to get to know a professor is to go to her office regularly during office hours. If you have a conflict with the professor's scheduled office hours, ask if there is another time she is available to meet. Be sure to have read the materials or worked through the assigned problems, and go prepared with questions and comments. A final way to get a professor to know you is to participate in class frequently.

Engage with residential campus life.

College is about more than the academic experience. It's important to be engaged and involved in campus life. Students who are involved in clubs, sports, pre-professional activities, and volunteer work tend to be happier at college and (as you would expect) more connected with others. These experiences can help young adults to grow socially and to connect with people from different backgrounds. They also give students an opportunity to explore areas of interest, develop a passion, and pursue an involvement that could lead to a career. Students who want to get an "Ivy League" education at their college should make full use of the resources and nonacademic opportunities on campus.

They might join a startup club to learn about the entrepreneurial process, a computer programming club to learn to code, an EMT group to provide emergency care, or a community-service club to help others and develop new perspectives about the world. Some students perform with arts organizations, play club sports, or write for the campus media.

The University of Texas at Austin, one of the largest universities in the United States, has more than nine hundred campus organizations. Other colleges tend to have no fewer than several hundred, so there is ample opportunity for all students to get involved, to learn, and to lead. Even fun clubs are positive, because they get students connected to one another and expose them to new people. The Georgetown University Grilling Society is a group of students who grill hundreds of burgers for the campus community on the main lawn every Friday. Students have fun, bring the community together, and can earn rankings such as "Grill Master" and "Grill Sergeant." Campus clubs represent an opportunity to try something new, develop a skill or interest, make new friends, and enjoy the college experience.

STEP 4: DEVELOP SKILLS AND ROUTINES THAT HELP YOU ADAPT AND EXCEL AT COLLEGE.

New freshmen have suddenly moved away from everything familiar to them—family, friends, home, community—and are beginning to make their way as adults while surrounded by strangers in a new setting. They may feel that everything is on the line and question their ability to succeed at college-level work, build adult relationships, and live away from home. They have an increase in personal freedom and personal responsibility, new time management challenges, and additional academic pressures, and they must adjust to life with a roommate and changing relationships with family and friends at home.

A 2013 survey of 123,000 college students on 153 campuses found that half feel overwhelming anxiety and one-third experience depression sometime during a typical school year.[81] Emotional challenges have the potential to quickly derail a college career, so it is important for students to develop skills that will help keep them happy and in control. Parents should talk with their children about the changes they will face and discuss potential solutions and strategies. They should not underestimate the challenges of freshman year and should not tell their children that it will be the best year of their lives.

Students with strong emotional intelligence and social skills may know what they need to do in order to ensure a good adjustment. Others may need to consider new routines, actions, and skills to help them get through the first year successfully, such as the following:

> ▶ **Get connected to the right people:** Make friends with people who take school seriously and are supportive. Be wary of "party friends." Get to know your advisor and any other professors or coaches who might become mentors. If you need to talk with someone at the counseling center or a private therapist, don't hesitate to get those professional relationships established.
> ▶ **Be physically well:** Keep a healthy schedule with plenty of time for sleep, exercise, and downtime. Eat well and don't get involved with binge drinking.

▶ **Get involved:** Join clubs and/or activities, volunteer, and reach out to others in your dorm or classes.

▶ **Get organized:** Plan your weekly schedule and include study hours. Make "to do" lists or keep an organized planner.

▶ **Manage your emotions:** Online newsmagazine *College Parent Central* identified four keys to managing emotions that have been helpful to college students as they navigate their new lives on campus:[82]

    ▪ **Monitor:** Pay attention to how you feel at various times. Notice when your moods change in positive or negative directions. Just paying attention may help you understand how you are feeling.

    ▪ **Label:** Try to identify what you are feeling. Identifying and putting a name to an emotion is a good first step to dealing with it.

    ▪ **Determine:** Once you have noticed how you are feeling and given it a label, try to figure out what has caused the emotion. Did a particular event cause the emotional change? Is it related to a class or activity or person? Just knowing why you experience an emotion may help you cope with it.

    ▪ **Manage:** If you can notice a mood, label it, and determine its cause, you are in a better position to try to manage that emotion. You may simply need to let it run its course, but you may also be able to work to change the way that you feel. You can talk to friends, a resident assistant, an advisor, or a counselor.

▶ **Adjust your expectations:** Just because you heard that college is supposed to be the best time of your life, don't get down because it doesn't feel that way. Adjustment takes time, and lasting friendships take a while to build.

STEP 5: FOCUS ON PAID EMPLOYMENT AND INTERNSHIPS.

Don't underestimate the value of paid work of any kind. Young adults may look down on retail, food service, work-study, or camp counseling jobs, but these actually provide a chance to build skills and confidence, gain experience, and get a taste of responsibility. Paid work gives students a sense of contributing to a greater effort and to helping others. It can also demonstrate to potential employers a greater level of maturity and financial responsibility. And, of course, most students can use the money, and for many a student job is crucial to thriving financially while in college. A director of recruitment at an investment bank told me, "Sometimes I see internships on a resume but no paid work so I ask them if they have ever held a paying job. If they are college seniors and have never worked for pay, it gives me pause."

ANDREW WHITE: BUILDING JOB SKILLS AND CONNECTIONS DURING COLLEGE

 Andrew White had clear goals for his college experience before he started his freshman year at Virginia Tech. Andrew's dream job is to be a chief financial officer of an NBA basketball team. His goal for college is to gain an understanding of finance and business through studying in the university's undergraduate business school, but also to get exposure to the business side of sports in any way possible.

Andrew is no stranger to the business of sports, as he already had three sports-related internships before he finished high school. He interned at InTennis, Women on Course, and the Mid-Atlantic Sports Network, and each experience gave him valuable insight into a different side of the sports world. Andrew got the internships through one valuable personal connection—a family friend—who introduced him to these opportunities. Like many ambitious high school students, Andrew had a LinkedIn account, which he set up during eleventh grade.

At the end of his freshman year, Andrew got a coveted student manager position with the Virginia Tech men's basketball team. The position wasn't listed at the career center, and he did not apply online. Andrew knew that Coach Buzz Williams had left Marquette to become the new head coach of Virginia Tech. From his dorm room window, he saw boxes being moved into the athletic center, and he recognized Coach Williams from television. He hurried over to the athletic center and offered to help the coach move into his new office. He spent several hours moving boxes and doing errands for the coach to help him get settled in. By the end of the day, Coach Williams offered Andrew the student manager job, and he accepted.

Andrew stayed on at Virginia Tech during the summer to help with player workouts, office work, and recruiting. The hours are long, and there is no pay in the first year, but he hopes to qualify for a student manager scholarship in his second year. Andrew says that the internship is hard work but extremely rewarding, and he loves being involved in the inner workings of a Division I basketball program. He enjoys traveling with the team, making connections in the basketball world, and furthering his progress toward his long-term goals.

A good internship has become the touchstone for a top-quality college experience. Internships are highly coveted, often elusive, and probably the biggest topic of chatter among college students and their parents. Everyone in the family keeps their eyes and ears open for news of a potential internship. A survey by the National Association of Colleges and Employers found that nearly two-thirds of the class of 2013 had internship or co-op experience.[83] Co-ops combine classroom education with practical work experience, with the student getting credit (and sometimes pay, too) for the work. From the employer's point of view, a resume with internship or co-op experience is generally stronger and more likely to lead to a full-time job. Philip D. Gardner, research director of the Collegiate Employment Research Institute, says that internship experience is "just one of those things you have to have before employers will even consider looking at your resume."[84]

The website InternMatch conducted a survey of more than nine thousand college students and noted two interesting things about how internships relate to getting that first job: First, paid internships have more value than unpaid internships. Students with paid internships were three times more likely to have received job offers than students with unpaid internships. Second, resumes with several internships were more impressive than those with only one internship. Students with three or more internships were twice as likely to have received a job offer as those with only one internship.[85]

Bottom line: aim for paid work and internships (but if you are able to and haven't found an internship that pays, take one that doesn't). See Chapter Eight for an in-depth discussion of the job and internship search.

STEP 6: DEVELOP COMMUNICATION SKILLS, BOTH WRITTEN AND SPOKEN.

As college students leave their teens and enter young adulthood, it's important that their speaking, body language, and other communication skills mature with them. One would certainly question the intelligence and job-readiness of a young adult who talks like a twelve-year-old, and yet many young adults have not developed a professional presentation and don't seem to understand how important it is.

Trouble areas, which can be improved with determination and focus, include using filler words and slang, speaking before thinking, writing emails using texting language, and using "up talk." The term *up talk* refers to speaking with a high-rising terminal syllable at the end of a sentence, which makes the sentence sound like a question. This can connote apology or uncertainty, even when neither is intended. Many teens unconsciously use up talk, and they often speak in sentences that are littered with slang and filler words, such as *like, you know, um, uh, sure,* and *okay.* If they make a conscious choice to avoid these words and sounds, and listen carefully to people they know who do not use them, they can improve.

A few of my clients have improved their professional presentations by giving campus tours at their colleges. They had a captive audience to listen to them talk for almost an hour on a topic they knew well. With each tour, they tried to eliminate up talk, slang, and filler words as much as they could. They also benefitted from the question-and-answer session, during which they had to respond to questions from parents and students. Students who are unable to give tours can try mock interview sessions at their career-services centers; they may benefit from watching a recording of their session. Other students report the benefit of "studying" the speech patterns of adults who they know and admire. One of my clients improved her professional presentation by watching old, classic movies. She saw examples of people speaking clearly, in full sentences, with great confidence, and she tried to replicate it.

Texting is a language unto itself and not one that should be carried into the professional world. Students developing their professional presentation should practice writing emails. Whether they are writing to a professor, a potential employer, or an adult friend or colleague, it's important to use a greeting, full sentences, and a closing, and to check for spelling mistakes, awkward sentence structure, and any other errors before sending it.

For a few more helpful communication hints as you prepare yourself for interviews, see page 115.

STEP 7: WORK IN A TEAM. IF POSSIBLE, LEAD A TEAM.

Teamwork is more than just a twenty-first-century buzzword. The modern workplace requires collaboration, and employers prefer candidates who can cite examples of times that they have contributed to a team, led a team, or mediated a conflict on a team. Students can get experience working on a team through on-campus student organizations, such as student government, clubs, campus publications, and even sororities and fraternities. If these groups offer an opportunity to run an event, lead a new initiative, or run for an officer position, take it! Young adults can also get teamwork experience through jobs, internships, and class projects. College students need to be deliberate in the way that they chose activities, jobs, and classes so that they are able to develop the team experience that is so crucial in today's workplace.

STEP 8: STEP OUT OF YOUR COMFORT ZONE.

We learn the most from the people who are most unlike us. Whether they come from a different part of the world or a different culture or they just have a different point of view, we benefit from knowing them. College campuses are full of students with unique backgrounds and varied interests and beliefs, and all students should make a point of branching out and getting to know people who are different from themselves. Even though it may seem that international students spend the most time with people from their home countries, they have chosen to attend school in another country for a reason—often for a taste of the country's culture—and are usually very open to meeting those who extend an offer of friendship, or at least an invitation for a cup of coffee.

Study abroad also offers the opportunity to experience another culture and country firsthand, which is especially valuable in today's global economy. Students can improve language skills, learn about regional politics or customs, and experience life in an international university setting. Young adults learn things about the world that they could not have learned at home; they understand the world from a much wider perspective and see it in a new and different way. Only 1 percent of American college students study abroad. In Britain, 1.7 percent of students study abroad, and 1.4 percent of students in India and China do so.[86] However, 57 percent of Georgetown students study abroad, as do 55 percent from Princeton, 51 percent from Stanford, and 50 percent from Dartmouth. Elite college students study abroad at a rate fifty times higher than that of the average college student. Of course, you don't need to attend an Ivy League college to study abroad; it is an opportunity open to everyone, and something that anyone who wants "Ivy League" value should consider.

One of the most important attributes for a young person to have today is a global consciousness: an understanding of other cultures and a concern for issues in the wider world. A person with language skills or insight into another region is a valuable asset for any company. So why do so many college students study language, culture, and politics from their home campus rather than going abroad?

There is a misconception that study abroad is prohibitively expensive for most students. Actually, a year abroad can cost half as much as a year at your home campus. If you enroll directly in a university abroad rather than using a study-abroad program, you may pay very little. Students enrolling directly in universities in Norway and Germany have no tuition costs, and those in Finland and Austria have very low fees, under $5,000 a year. But even if you do use a study-abroad company, you are likely to find that most programs are less expensive than a private American university. Butler University's Institute for Study Abroad has many well-run programs priced at around $30,000 a year, including room and board, with some as low as $20,000 a year. For those paying $60,000 a year in tuition to their private US colleges, a year abroad represents a significant cost savings and an exciting educational adventure.

Financial aid is provided for students who study abroad, although different study-abroad programs provide different types and amounts of aid. A student who enrolls in a program sponsored by her own university often has no change in financial-aid status. Some colleges offer departmental grants or additional loans to students who are facing higher college expenses due to studying abroad.

A semester or year abroad can offer an opportunity to broaden your worldview. However, students who can't leave their home campuses during the school year should not give up on having an international experience. Student-athletes and those with campus jobs or leadership roles in student organizations are often unable to spend a semester or a year at another university, but these students can consider a shorter study trip during the summer or during a school vacation. Young people who are curious about the world and open to developing a unique worldview can also find things to do on their own campuses, such as studying a foreign language, joining campus cultural groups, and making friends with students from abroad.

Dr. Allan Goodman, president of the Institute of International Education, noted, "The careers of all of our students will be global ones, in which they will need to function effectively in multi-national teams. They will need to understand the cultural differences and historical experiences that divide us, as well as the common values and humanity that unite us."[87] To prepare for these careers, abandoning the comfort zone is vital.

Putting the Success Profile to Work: How to Get a Great Job After (or During) College

Let's face it: most stress about college admissions is rooted in the desire for a successful career. Although there is a lot of talk about finding the "perfect-fit" college and the right campus environment, when I talk with parents about college admissions, there is a big focus on helping their child's career prospects. If a top college means a better chance at a fulfilling career, many parents are willing to try anything or pay any tuition amount to make it happen.

"I just want him to stay in the upper middle class," one parent admitted to me. "It's tough out there, and I see so many kids moving back home with no job, or with a low-paying job. I've become focused on trying to get him into a good college because I want to do whatever I can for him." Likewise, lower-income families see an elite college as a way to increase their children's social mobility. "She'll have more opportunities if she goes to a well-known college," one lower-income parent said to me. "The payback will come later, when she has a great career."

Another parent, who had limited her son's college search to campuses within a four-hour drive of her New Jersey home, suddenly relented and allowed him to attend his first-choice college in Texas. "I did some research," she said, "And the economy is much stronger in Texas. There are lots of jobs in Houston. If he can go there and get a career going and make a life for himself, I'm okay with it. I think he may have a better chance there."

With all the news about the economic hardships facing recent college graduates, parents certainly should be worried. A Harvard study found that just 62.9 percent of Millennials (those under age 30) are currently employed, and half of them are only working part-time.[88] Pew Research and the US Census found that 21.6 million adults, or 36 percent of the age eighteen to thirty-one population, are living at home with their parents, the highest level in over four decades. Of course, some of them are college students, but 16 percent of the population aged twenty-five to thirty-one is living in the parental home.[89] With reports showing 250 resumes submitted for every corporate job,[90] parents wonder what they can do to position their children for success.

Parental worry does not discriminate. Parents of all economic backgrounds, with struggling as well as high-achieving students, bring their worry with them to college admissions meetings. They come with stories about how difficult it is to get hired on Wall Street, in technology, and even in teaching and public relations. Most of them conclude that the best way to increase their children's chances of meaningful employment would be to get them into the highest-ranked college possible.

But of course, the reality is that graduating from an expensive or prestigious college may not make much of a difference in the job search. We have reviewed statistics on graduates' earnings that suggest that those at elite colleges won't make any more than if they had attended moderately selective colleges (see page 26). We can also look at leaders in various fields and see that many types of colleges are represented. And while there are some industries, such as investment banking and consulting, that do favor elite-college graduates, for the majority of employers, the name brand of the college is not a major factor.

If employers aren't hiring individuals based on the perceived quality of their colleges, then what are they looking for? Much of it is intimately connected with the Success Profile.

QUALITIES THAT EMPLOYERS VALUE IN COLLEGE GRADUATES

Several studies and articles in the news have shown that salaries are correlated to college majors, which leads some people to conclude that the choice of major is the biggest factor in career financial success.[91] We can see that engineering majors tend to make more than philosophy majors, so it seems like the smart thing is to major in something "practical." Many students feel compelled to study pre-professional subjects, such as business, engineering, computer science, or health sciences, because they think that employers are turned off by liberal-arts majors such as English, psychology, and history. However, according to several recent employer surveys, a person's long-term professional success depends more on having the right skills for the workplace than having had a specific major.

The American Association of Colleges and Universities surveyed 318 employers in businesses and non-profits about qualities and skills that they valued in recent college graduates. Almost all of the employers (93 percent) said that "a demonstrated capacity to think critically, communicate clearly, and solve complex problems is more important than [a candidate's] undergraduate major."[92] The majority of the employers said they wanted college students to place more emphasis in these key areas: critical thinking, complex problem-solving, written and oral communication, and applied knowledge in real-world settings. It's important for students to realize this early, since these qualities that employers so clearly want are things that they must develop over time. It isn't enough to try to brush up on these skills before job interviews. Students need to have a career focus and a plan for developing these skills before and during the college years. Following the steps described in Chapter 5 (page 65) is an excellent way to develop them. Even students majoring in engineering or computer science have to develop these skills, since even employers hiring STEM types give preference to those with strong critical-thinking and communication skills.

The employers in the survey also indicated that it was important for job candidates to demonstrate ethical judgment and integrity, intercultural skills, and the capacity for continued learning. They also felt that all college students, regardless of their major, should acquire broad knowledge in the liberal arts and sciences.

An especially interesting finding of the survey was that four out of five employers said that an electronic portfolio would be useful when evaluating candidates.[93] In Chapter 11, we will discuss some other potential changes to colleges' offerings and employers' expectations. Job applicants are going to have to show more than just a college degree and resume to potential employers. They are going to have to demonstrate the skills and knowledge they have gained that will help them to progress at the company if they are hired.

The National Association of Colleges and Employers conducted its own survey of more than two hundred hiring firms, asking them to rate job candidates' skills and qualities. The survey found that the most important quality was a candidate's ability to work in a team structure. The next two highest-rated qualities were decision-making and problem-solving abilities, followed by the ability to plan, organize, and prioritize work. The fourth most important skill was the ability to verbally communicate with people both inside and outside the organization. These "soft skills" were at the top of the survey, ahead of "technical knowledge related to the job" and "proficiency with computer software programs," which were rated seventh and eighth.[94]

In one final poll, conducted by Peter D. Hart Research Associates, about what preparation colleges should give their students, employers listed many of the skills described above, along with "the ability to apply knowledge and skills in new settings" and an understanding of not only science, technology, numbers, and statistics, but also the "global context in which work is now done."[95]

A student reading about the importance of soft skills might be quick to think that he is strong in these areas and that this isn't a concern for him. Maybe he enjoys people and feels that he would be a good element of a team. However, it isn't enough that he feels this; he also has to be able to demonstrate it in an interview. He could be asked, "Tell me about a team project that you've worked on," or "Tell me about a time you stepped into a leadership role on a team." There are college students who cannot answer these questions because they haven't had the opportunity to work in a team while in college. They are clearly at a disadvantage. But if the student has focused on developing his Success Profile for years prior to his job search, he won't have this problem. Knowing the importance of showing his ability to work on a team, the student will have selected classes with group projects, jobs or internships that involved teamwork, and/or extracurricular activities on campus that could give him this type of experience. Whether it is teamwork, critical thinking, or communication skills, it's important for students to cultivate the qualities that are in demand for companies that will be their potential employers.

PUTTING YOUR BEST FOOT FORWARD

Preparation for the job search starts long before the senior year of college. There are many things a student can and should do to increase her chances for success. The following are tips and ideas for developing a background that is appealing to hiring managers. (If you've already been working on your Success Profile, much of this will be review!)

- ▶ Employers look at both grades and course selection, and they may review your entire transcript. It is important to be purposeful in the way that you select your courses. Do your best to select relevant classes and to achieve good grades.
- ▶ Students can get valuable experience by being involved in groups or activities on campus. Writing for the school newspaper, organizing a charity event for your sorority, volunteering in the community, and playing on a sports team are all helpful additions to your resume. They are also good interview fodder, since you can discuss your experiences working with a diverse group of people, setting a goal and working toward it, and learning new skills.
- ▶ International experience is highly valued by employers, so if you have the chance to study abroad, even for a short time, take it. Likewise, fluency in another language will be impressive to many employers.
- ▶ Career-related experience helps students to gain insight into a field and let employers know that they are serious candidates. This can, of course, be an internship, which is the holy grail of career preparation and is highlighted on page 131. But there are many other career-related activities that can be

valuable for young adults. College students can join pre-professional clubs on campus in an area of interest, such as the Investment Management Association, Pre-Law Society, Biological Engineering Club, or Computer Programmers Club, and if they are smart, they will try to take on a leadership role. Another excellent way to get exposure to your field of interest is to ask for informational meetings with people employed in these areas. Those who want to get some practical experience may be able to volunteer, do a class project, or study in the field of interest.

▶ College students can register with the campus career-planning services office, where they can talk with a career counselor, attend guest speaker presentations, participate in workshops, and do research on fields of interest, in addition to searching through the center's job and internship listings

▶ Networking, establishing a *professional* social-media presence, and having a professional presentation are crucial for today's job search

▶ Don't underestimate the value of a paid job, whether it relates to your career interest or not. Some employers will not consider a college graduate who has never worked for pay.

▶ Distinguish yourself by doing one thing that makes you very different from everyone else. Whether it is a quirky hobby, a great achievement, or a unique cultural connection, it can help you stand out in a competitive job market.

TOP 10 INTERVIEW QUESTIONS FOR RECENT GRADUATES

University of Virginia career services offered these sample interview questions and insights (plus ten others) on its Career Services website.

1. *Tell me about yourself.*

- EMPLOYER MOTIVATION: To see how well you can communicate and structure your thoughts.
- STRATEGY: Prepare for this question in advance. Pretend that the employer said "Tell me about yourself and why you are interested in this job." You might respond by quickly mentioning your relevant background, experience, and skills and then explaining why you believe that the job would be the next logical step for you.

2. *"What are your greatest work and non-work accomplishments?"*

- EMPLOYER MOTIVATION: To know what you care about and what motivates you.
- STRATEGY: Choose something about which you are passionate. Do not say "Getting into (your college)."

3. *"Describe three things that have been most important to you in a job."*

- EMPLOYER MOTIVATION: To find out about your work-related values.
- STRATEGY: Be truthful about what matters to you professionally rather than personally.

Sidebar Continues

4. *"How did you prepare for this interview?"*

- EMPLOYER MOTIVATION: To see if you have made an effort to research the company, an indicator of your interest and initiative.
- STRATEGY: Talk about any research that you've done through the company website, news articles, employees of the company, etc.

5. *"What do you know about this organization?"*

- EMPLOYER MOTIVATION: Similar to the previous question, the employer is checking your knowledge base and interest.
- STRATEGY: Provide an answer that indicates that you have researched the company before the interview. Example: "I've talked with some of your employees, and they feel that this a good company to work for because..." "I've been reading that your company is really growing fast, planning two new branches this year. I want to work for your company because the future looks promising."

6. *"What are three of your biggest strengths and three of your biggest weaknesses?"*

- EMPLOYER MOTIVATION: To find out if your strengths would be used in the position and to find out if you are aware of the areas where you need improvement.
- STRATEGY: Provide specific examples of your strengths (e.g., "I'm an excellent writer. Most of my teachers have commented on my ability to organize my thoughts and communicate with a variety of audiences.") With your weaknesses, explain how you work around them or try to strengthen them. Avoid sharing a weakness that directly relates to the job's requirements.

7. *"Why did you choose your major?"*

- EMPLOYER MOTIVATION: To assess your teamwork, interpersonal, and leadership skills.
- STRATEGY: Be open about your interests. Consider what aspects of your interests are most relevant to the job, and focus on that side (e.g. your love of independent quantitative analysis vs. your love of team projects).

8. *"Tell me about a time when you worked as part of a team."*

- EXPLORER MOTIVATION: To assess your teamwork, interpersonal, and leadership skills.
- STRATEGY: Pick a specific example that has a "happy ending" and about which you are proud.

9. *"What specific skills have you acquired or used in previous jobs that relate to this position?"*

- EMPLOYER MOTIVATION: To see if you have a clear idea of the skills needed for the advertised position.
- STRATEGY: Be sure to have thought about your skills before the interview. A good way to do this is to highlight the skills mentioned in the job description and then think about how you might be able to prove each of those skills.

10. *"How would you motivate a co-worker who was performing poorly on a team project?"*

- EMPLOYER MOTIVATION: To see how you relate to others and perhaps how you can think outside the box.
- STRATEGY: Draw upon your teamwork experiences, both school- and work-related, to present a thoughtful and logical approach.

Source: University of Virginia Career Services, http://www.career. virginia.edu/students/handouts/interviewing.pdf

THE IMPORTANCE OF CULTURAL FIT

Companies today are looking for employees who are a good "cultural fit" for their organizations, knowing that people who are a match for their corporate culture are more likely to be productive and stay in the job longer. They feel that the best way to hedge against the job-hopping tendencies of young professionals is to screen carefully for cultural fit. Likewise, recent graduates are evaluating companies with an eye to a firm's culture, evaluating if and how they would fit in. A recent study from Millennial Branding and Beyond.com found that 43 percent of human-resources professionals rank "cultural fit" as the single most important thing in the hiring process, followed by "relevant courses" (21 percent) and "internship experience" (13 percent).[96]

"Cultural fit" means a match between the firm and the employee in regard to values, behaviors, work habits, and even personality. The good news is that there are opportunities for a candidate to assess a firm's corporate culture through research and meetings. Students can search their LinkedIn network or college alumni database for individuals who work at the firms they are interested in. They can contact these people and ask them to meet for coffee or an informational meeting to discuss their experiences working at the company. They can also research firm culture through websites such as www.vault.com and www.glassdoor.com, both of which offer insight from current and past employees of thousands of firms. Finally, many companies showcase their people and day-to-day operations by posting work-life stories, biographies of employees, daily-life schedules, videos and interviews, and details on projects and assignments on their websites. While this information has been crafted by the firm, it does offer some insight into daily life there.

A company with a rigid hierarchy would not be a good fit

for a candidate who wants to have his opinions and ideas valued or considered immediately. A person who needs a calm and quiet environment might not perform as well at a firm that is heavy on collaboration and has a big open workspace instead of private offices or cubicles. Companies that require long working hours need to find employees who are not only willing to take that on, but who also thrive under high pressure and with limited free time. A candidate who is more traditional and likes to have work assigned to her may not excel in a creative office that is less "task-oriented." These are just a few examples of the variety of working environments and corporate cultures found across industries today.

Cultural fit can also come down to something as simple as a personality match with supervisor and co-workers. Students should be prepared to be open and authentic in their interviews. They should remember all of their preparation and training for the interviews, but also keep the conversation natural and upbeat.

The Millennial Branding and Beyond.com survey also found that 84 percent of hiring managers were looking for candidates with a positive attitude. That fact shouldn't come as a surprise; what is surprising is that 33 percent of hiring managers had recently interviewed a candidate who they rated as having a "bad attitude." Certainly, there are few if any companies whose official cultural fit includes bad attitude. Students going into an interview situation should remember to do their best to stay positive and confident during the interview.

INTERNSHIPS: THE GOLDEN TICKET OF JOB PREPARATION

In the summer of 2014, almost ninety thousand students applied for a summer internship at one firm: Morgan Stanley. The lucky one thousand students who were selected for these highly paid and highly coveted internships have very strong shots at full-time employment at the firm and a great start to a career in banking. Morgan Stanley's CEO, James Gorman, said, "We hope that after graduation [the summer analysts and associates] will join our full-time programs as the newest generation of talented professionals at our firm."[97] More than ever, internships offer a fast-track path to jobs, making them essential for students who are serious about finding good jobs after graduation.

On page 112, we discussed the importance of internships (especially paid ones) and part-time jobs. It's important to look at the internship search process as the starting point for the full-time job search. It's never too early to start building relationships that can lead to future internships or jobs. It's also never too early to start researching career options, companies, and entry-level roles, or to try to get experience and build knowledge any way you can.

It's tempting for students to limit their internship search to job boards and their college's Career Services office's internship listings. Using these sources doesn't involve anything more taxing than reading internship descriptions and sending a resume and cover letter. While these sources can lead to jobs, it's important to look beyond that and be more aggressive in the internship search.

Students can connect with people through LinkedIn or set up informational meetings, over coffee or otherwise, with adults working in fields of interest to better understand a company, its industry, and the different roles of the players involved. They can also research opportunities at local companies or offer their service as an intern to smaller firms that don't have a formal internship program.

Competition is stiff at the big-name companies. For example, *The New York Times* reported that ten thousand students applied for just ninety summer internships at ESPN in 2010.[98] There are better odds at smaller firms and local companies. If you are interested in journalism, apply for an internship at your local paper or newsroom. Research companies in your field of interest in smaller cities, and remember that your personal contacts and relationships are your best introduction to a new company.

The Career Services offices are a great resource for mock interviews, research, and consultations on interview attire. Staff members might be able to connect you with alumni who work in your field of interest.

Popular job boards, such as www.internmatch.com and www.internships.com, have thousands of listings, but also offer good opportunities that help you learn about the role of an intern in various companies and can be a great research source. There are also industry-specific job boards, such as Mediabistro for journalism, Book Jobs for publishing, Idealist for non-profits, and Dice.com for technology professionals.

DEVELOP A PROFESSIONAL SOCIAL MEDIA PRESENCE

Most college students have already heard about how important it is to clean up their Facebook pages or any other social-media sites that have pictures or comments that they wouldn't want an employer to see. But many young adults don't realize that a large amount of their networking and research should be conducted online as well.

A few years ago, I was surprised when I got LinkedIn connection requests from my teenage clients. But now it is the norm to have a LinkedIn account in college, and many ambitious high school students have them as well. Students can start by connecting with adults who they know, either through school, family, or outside activities. They will continue to build on these connections as they go through college and into the workforce. A LinkedIn presence also makes a student visible to hiring managers, who often search for candidates online and look at their profiles and connections. Students can develop their connections by leveraging all the relationships in their network, including parents, older siblings, friends, relatives, teachers, and coaches.

CareerBuilder conducted a recent survey that asked employers why they used social networks to research job candidates. The main reason cited was a desire to see if the prospective employee presented himself professionally, but half of responders also said that they used the social network to see if the candidate would be a good fit for the company culture. It's important for students to understand that developing a professional social media presence means so much more than just cleaning up their Facebook page. Employers will be evaluating Facebook, LinkedIn, and Twitter accounts to learn more about the candidate and her potential.

In an "Ask the Interviewers" section of its careers website, Goldman Sachs recommends applicants follow Goldman on Twitter and LinkedIn. The Goldman Sachs interviewer says, "That could demonstrate real interest, especially if someone knows the subject matter of what we've been tweeting—that could make for great conversation in an interview."

The importance of social media in the job search is not limited to financial-services firms. Chris Hoyt, talent engagement and marketing leader at PepsiCo, said in an interview with StartWire, "While resumes are still important, they're not necessarily what a sourcer or recruiter is going to see first. Job seekers that manage their online footprint, how they are portrayed and how they're engaged, on various social and professional networks like Twitter or LinkedIn could find it makes all the difference."[99]

CONSIDER GRADUATE SCHOOL

A graduate degree is mandatory in some fields, so students who hope to become doctors, lawyers, or academics, for example, know that they will attend graduate school. Other fields, such as business, education, engineering, science research, and journalism, include professionals who have graduate degrees, but the credential is not always mandatory. Most young adults who consider graduate school also have to consider when to attend. It is no longer the norm to go to graduate school directly after college. In fact, most MBA programs require three or more years of work experience, and many law students work for a year before starting their degrees. Students who have been developing their Success Profile will find that their skills and experiences will help them not only to be admitted to a graduate program, but to excel there as well.

Like undergraduate colleges, graduate schools seek to put together a diverse class of students from all over the country and the world. They don't favor students who attended selective colleges, but instead look at the individual student's grades, testing, and accomplishments. For example, Harvard Business School accepts students from far beyond the top fifty most elite colleges, with its class of 2015 hailing from 264 different colleges. Likewise, Harvard Law enrolled students from 171 colleges, and Yale Law's two hundred members of the class of 2017 came from 77 different undergraduate institutions. Washington University School of Medicine selected its 123 incoming students from seventy colleges, showing that the committee gave little to no preference to elite colleges.

THE JOB SEARCH PROCESS

A successful job search is one that is multifaceted, creative, and networking-focused. Students can start by establishing their online profiles, writing their resume, and having both reviewed by career center staff. They can also practice interviewing and spend some time reviewing lists of questions typically asked in their fields of interest. The next important step is one that many college students like to avoid: they should approach people in their field and ask to meet with them to discuss their jobs. These people can be alumni from their college, their parents' friends, LinkedIn connections, or a colleague they've met through a previous job or internship. These meetings give students valuable exposure to a field while also making potential connections for a job or internship.

Although students should not limit their job search to online job boards, the boards can be effective tools. The Millennial Branding study discussed earlier found that 45 percent of human resources professionals find candidates on job boards; the next-most common sources were the companies' own websites (18 percent) and employee referrals (17 percent)—although 71 percent of the employers said that referral candidates get high priority when deciding whom to hire.[100]

Students should be creative while job hunting. They should expand their searches outside the Career Services offices' job listings and the online boards by networking. Job fairs sponsored by college career services offices are a great way to bring applicants and employers together, and some forward-thinking colleges have been hosting virtual career fairs, where hiring managers chat with students online. Students should also research smaller markets: rather than being one of ninety thousand applying to work at Morgan Stanley, look for midsized investment banks in markets outside New York. If you want to go into advertising but can't get the attention of any big firms, try doing an ad project pro bono for a local non-profit. Contact a local advertising firm, ask for an informational interview, and bring your portfolio. When the competition is great, it's important to do what others are not doing.

Many successful job seekers keep a log of all the jobs they have applied to, which also lists follow-up emails or calls with interviewers or human-resources staff. Don't underestimate the value of persistence, following up, and going above and beyond.

When the search finally leads to an actual interview, the candidate should do a victory dance, and then move on to extensive research on the company and industry. It's important to be prepared. Too many students go into interviews knowing very little about the company, the job function, or the field of business. The student should make it his job to research extensively, get to know the corporate culture, talk to employees in her network who work at that firm, and show up at the interview with a good attitude and a positive outlook.

BEATING THE ODDS: THE SCOOP ON HARD-TO-GET JOBS

There is no magic formula for getting a job at the most sought-after firms in America. Recent college graduates rate Google as the most desirable place to work, and technology firms such as Apple, Qualcomm, and Microsoft are other hot destinations. Investment banks such as Goldman Sachs and Morgan Stanley, consulting firms like McKinsey and Bain, and consumer-goods companies, including Eli Lilly, Procter & Gamble, and GM, offer quality intern programs that are in high demand. There is no easy way into these firms, but here is some insight:

Gayle Laakmann McDowell was one of Microsoft's young-est interns. She moved up the ranks there and at Apple and Google. She published two books, *The Google Interview* and *Cracking the Coding Interview*, which are must-reads for anyone trying to get hired by technology firms. McDowell offers a few suggestions for wannabe Google interns. She advises that ap-plicants start something of their own: a small technology busi-ness or a project of another kind. It shows interviewers that a candidate has a passion for technology, expertise, and creativ-ity. She also recommends an online portfolio that provides details on a candidate's accomplishments and interests. Finally, she recommends getting out from behind the com-puter and going to tech events to meet people.

Edith Cooper, global head of Human Capital at Goldman Sachs, spoke to *Fortune* about the firm's entry-level hiring pro-gram. "We define talent very broadly," she said, and indicated that Goldman Sachs looks for candidates who have a stellar track record in some field outside academics. They also like applicants who have shown leadership in a number of different contexts, including sports, jobs, volunteerism, other extracur-ricular activities, and class projects. Goldman Sachs employees are passionate and curious about the financial markets, so it is crucial for candidates to demonstrate their own interest in the financial markets and be able to talk about them extensively. Students who have a contrarian opinion or a unique insight may have a special edge in the recruiting process.[101]

One field that has even worse odds than Wall Street or technology is broadcasting. If your ultimate goal is to be-come a network anchor or a *60 Minutes* host, you may find yourself interviewing for jobs in smaller markets and still having trouble getting callbacks.

Dan Patrick, an Emmy-winning sportscaster, was with ESPN's Sports Center for eighteen years. He offered this ad-vice on ESPN.com to young people hoping to take over from him someday:

My first piece of advice would be to get a job at a newspaper, TV or radio station in any capacity. Preferably a job that involves writing and reporting. Once you are inside, you can hear about jobs that are opening before anyone else does. If you want to get into broadcasting, start in radio so you can develop a tape—then people can hear what you sound like and if you are knowledgeable. Constantly update the tape as you improve. Also, listen to your own work and critique it.[102]

Patrick further explains that it's not enough to be a sports fan and know your favorite teams and favorite sports. You have to be an actual student of the sports world, knowing about even the boring teams and less-popular sports and events.

As competitive as it is, broadcasting has plenty in common with other professions; for example, as Patrick comments, "Writing is essential. We write everything we say, so you have to learn how to express yourself creatively and intelligently and knowledgeably on a tight deadline."

A MEDIA TRAINER'S TIPS ON DEVELOPING YOUR PROFESSIONAL PRESENTATION

How you present yourself to the world matters. Employers want to hire young adults who speak and act professionally, and they look for evidence of this in the hiring process. Terri Trespicio offers tips on four personal-presentation problems that plague young adults today. Terri is a media personality who has hosted her own radio show, *Whole Living*, on Martha Stewart Radio, and has made frequent television appearances on *The Martha Stewart Show* and *The Today Show*, and she trains media personalities at 2 Market Media.

Sidebar Continues

1. The Vocal Pause

"Um" is a common one, but others include "so," "and," and "uh," or any combination thereof. The reason is simple: you're trying to kill time and fill the void while you think of something to say or complete a thought. The problem is that it adds no value to what you're saying and can be distracting for the person listening. In a way, what you're doing is saying, "Keep paying attention to me while I think."

> ■ TRY IT: Take a real pause. It's perfectly okay to have a moment of silence while you gather your thoughts. In fact, a pause can be quite powerful. It says that you're carefully considering what you say or what words you choose. It's the mark of a mature and unrushed speaker. Train yourself to allow that moment of silence, instead of struggling to fill it.

2. Overuse of "like"

Similar to the "um" problem, "like" can also be a space-filler when used to, like, I don't know, like, figure out what you want to say. (Sound familiar?) You say it to keep the momentum of your words going. The word "like" is a real word with a real use: When you say something is "like" something else, you're setting up a comparison. "It was like being in a nightmare." See? That's fine. But too many likes, and you're going to end up sounding like a ten-year-old ("I was like, no way, and like, so scared, and like..."). The real problem here is that it robs your words of power. You weren't "like" scared. You were scared!

> ■ TRY IT: Tune in to your habit. Pay attention to how often you use it as a crutch to get yourself through a sentence or story. You can't make

changes to your speech until you really know what you sound like. Try recording yourself sometime when you're chatting with friends, just to get a sense. To make a change, start to notice when you feel a "like" bubbling up, and drop it from the sentence. You'll find you don't actually need it. And it never made anyone sound smarter.

3. The "up-talk" question-sentence

This one is a pet peeve of mine because it undermines your power in a big way. The problem is, you don't hear yourself doing it. It's this upswing in tone at the end of sentences that makes everything you say sound like a question. "And then I went to meet a friend? Because she was having a really rough time? You know?" The reason you do it is because you're trying to get buy-in from the listener. You're making sure she's listening and understands you, even agrees with you, but in order to do that, you're asking your story instead of telling it.

■ TRY IT: Own it. When your statements sound like questions, the message is clear: you're not sure of yourself. You're either afraid to take a stand, or afraid someone will disagree with you. This is a mark of insecurity—and in fact the most powerful way to break the habit is to fake it till you make it. We have all felt a bit tentative about stating something in public. But you have to act confident in order to sound confident. This is less a vocal tweak than it is a psychological shift. You owe it to yourself to really own what you're saying, and that means ending statements with a period, not a question mark.

Sidebar Continues

4. The Insecurity Dance

You may not know this by name (because I made it up), but you have seen it done: it's the act of teetering around, moving, and shifting while you speak. Maybe it's when you're talking in front of the class or even an informal group of people—but what happens is you tuck one foot behind the other and teeter back and forth, shifting your weight. Or maybe you shift laterally, leaning on one leg and then the other. The reason you do it is obvious: you're nervous or uneasy, self-conscious and unsure. Whereas "um" is a verbal filler, this is a physical filler. You're literally filling space because you don't know what to do with yourself. It comes off as weak and unsure, and undermines your personal power.

- TRY IT: Plant your feet. This will feel weird, especially if you're used to the insecurity dance and the nervous itch of moving. Any theater teacher will tell you to move intentionally, with purpose. If you putter around, leaning and shifting and dancing about, you distract from what you're saying. Try standing still while you speak. Think of your feet as having roots deep into the ground, holding you strong. Someone who's capable of being still connotes far more power than someone who can't stand still. You can actually train yourself to feel more powerful by acting that way.

PART THREE

WHAT YOU *SHOULD*

CONSIDER WHEN

CHOOSING A

SCHOOL

Useful Criteria for Selecting a College

With more than 2,700 four-year colleges and universities in the United States, it is hard to know where to start when selecting a college. Rather than reviewing the rankings, investigating the familiar big names, or considering the colleges that your friends are going to, start by looking inward. Investigate your own interests, learning style, and preferences for campus life before you turn your attention to the colleges themselves. You will be more effective in critically evaluating colleges and making a well-reasoned decision if you use this framework for decision-making.

LOOK INWARD

Learning style

During your many years as a student, you have most likely learned about the academic conditions that help you to thrive. Are you a student who stays on task in classes that are heavy on discussion, or do you prefer lecture-based classes where you take in a lot of information on your own? Do you like small classes, or do you enjoy the diversity of opinions in a larger class? Have you benefitted from tutors, and is this one-on-one help an essential part of your success? Are you self-motivated, or do you need a little push? These are all things to consider when you determine the size of the college and the academic culture that will work best for you.

Academic interests

It's not unusual for a seventeen- or eighteen-year-old to be undecided about what he wants to study in college. In fact, one of the benefits of a traditional liberal-arts curriculum is that it leaves room to explore different subjects before deciding on a major. Students who are unsure about what they would like to study can think about possible career goals or about areas that will build their future job skills. Many benefit from taking a Strong Interest Inventory test, which helps students to evaluate careers and areas of interest.

Christina is a high school junior who told me that she only wanted to apply to undergraduate business programs, since she was excited to work for an international company someday. When asked what she liked about business or where she saw herself in the future, she mentioned interests in marketing, developing business plans, attending meetings, and working with people from all over the world. She took the Strong Interest Inventory, and the results said that she was Artistic and Social, which she agreed with. I showed her the typical undergraduate business curriculum, which includes classes in accounting, statistics, finance, and calculus, with few opportunities for creative or artistic classes. Christina decided that while she still wants a career in international business, she hasn't decided if an undergraduate business program is right for her. She is intrigued by classes in international relations and communications, so she has decided to stay open to different possibilities and not enroll in a structured undergraduate business program.

Other students have a clear goal for what they would like to study in college. Michael always loved English and writing and knew that college would be incomplete for him without a focus on literature, creative writing, and class discussions. Arpita knew that she wanted to study engineering because it was a good way to combine her interests in math and design. While it's not important that students have decided on a major or an area of academic interest, they should at least start considering their strengths, interests, and future career options in relation to the course of study they will pursue in college.

Financial means

It's never too early to start thinking about college financing. Parents and students should talk about available resources, their tolerance level for loans, and the amount of money they have available for college tuition before the student falls in love with an unaffordable option. Chapter 10 goes into much deeper detail about finding a financial fit.

Lifestyle and campus culture

The lifestyle consideration goes beyond whether you want a large or small college and how far away from home you're willing to go. Is your religion important enough to you that you want a campus environment that has religious traditions or a certain percentage of students who share your religious beliefs and customs? Do you want to attend a traditional university with Greek life, football games, and tailgating, or would you prefer a campus culture that de-emphasizes sports, or one that's somewhere in between? Many students have preferences for particular types of weather, and some need to be in the city, others in the country, and still others somewhere in between. If you have the luxury of leaving home for college, it's important to find a campus culture and environment that will help you thrive and be happy.

EVALUATE COLLEGES

Colleges for your learning style

Students who know how they learn best can evaluate colleges based on several academic factors. The student-to-faculty ratio and other indications of faculty accessibility are important considerations for all students, but especially for those who thrive on interaction with teachers. They can also look at class size and the availability of seminar-style classes. Students with learning disabilities or those who have benefitted from tutors and other one-on-one help should evaluate the learning support services offices at the colleges under consideration.

Academic programs on campus

Nearly all colleges offer an undecided option for freshmen, which allows them to explore several areas of study before deciding on a major. But young adults who are interested in professional majors that lead to specific careers have to find colleges that offer their subject of interest. Students who know that they want to study health sciences, nutrition, computer science, criminal justice, architecture, nursing, or graphic design have to look specifically for these majors when they evaluate colleges. There are colleges that offer majors in forensic science, video-game design, sustainability studies, fashion design, film, and digital media. Students who are seeking these unusual majors and courses of study have to include this criterion in their search, since they won't often find these majors.

Degree requirements are flexible at some colleges and more rigid at others. Some offer an open curriculum in which students have no requirements, while others have more structure: they might require writing, a level of foreign language proficiency, and a freshman seminar. Georgetown University's College of Arts & Sciences has established a core curriculum that is intended to cultivate intellectual skills of perception, analysis, interpretation, and expression. It requires two courses in each of the following subjects: philosophy, theology, history, math/science, and social science, as well as one writing course and intermediate proficiency in a foreign language. This is vastly different from a college like Brown University, which has an open curriculum and whose only requirement is two courses in writing.

Students who are evaluating academic programs should also consider the campus resources, support services, and strength of their major course of study at each school.

Financial analysis of your college choices

You can't consider college options without looking at cost and value. Chapter 10 covers this in detail.

Campus culture

It's not easy to get beyond the stereotypes and get to know what a particular campus is really like. Most colleges are diverse and broad places, where one person's experience might be completely different from that of his dorm-mate down the hall. It's important to look beyond general reputation and what you've heard from others, and to add your own perspective to your evaluation of student life and campus culture. See page 147 for suggestions on how to uncover the campus culture.

COLLEGES THAT CHANGE LIVES

Would you like to go to a college where the professors are not just teachers, but also mentors for life? Rather than sitting in large lecture theaters, would you like to have small classes with professors who are approachable, helpful, and understanding, with high expectations for their students? Loren Pope, a former *New York Times* education editor and student advocate, identified forty colleges with these characteristics and published the first edition of *Colleges That Change Lives* in 1996. These colleges have been known to offer students more than just a degree, but also a chance to improve skills and gain a sense of their own power to learn and succeed.

The colleges included in the book formed a nonprofit called Colleges That Change Lives, Inc., which has championed Pope's message and is a leading national advocate for quality collegiate academic experiences. CTCL is run by a volunteer board of directors and holds conferences all over the United States and in Asia and Latin America, where it promotes the organization's mission "to help students frame their search beyond the ratings and rankings and to find a college that cultivates a lifelong love of learning and provides the foundation for a successful and fulfilling life beyond college." The colleges are all small in size and are located throughout the country. They include St. John's College in Maryland, St. Olaf in Minnesota, the University of Puget Sound in Washington, Clark in

Massachusetts, Rhodes in Tennessee, and Lynchburg in Virginia. Students looking for a meaningful college experience with the chance to improve their skills in a close-knit academic community will find many good options among the Colleges That Change Lives.

Graduation rate

The graduate and freshman retention statistic offers a look inside a university to see how its students are doing. The National Center for Education Statistics found that 59 percent of full-time college students graduated within six years. On the high end, elite colleges show that 93 percent of entering students graduate within six years, and 96 percent of freshmen return the next year. Strong state schools like the University of Wisconsin-Madison report 83 percent of students graduating within six years and 95 percent of the freshmen returning. If you are interested in a college with a retention rate that is below the national average, it is worth further exploration to see if this is really the right college for you, or setting up a plan for support and success if you do enroll in a college with a low reported graduation rate.

Unique campus opportunities

Many students are drawn to a particular university because of the unique programs that it has established. Honors Colleges within a university often offer perks such as faculty mentors, small class size, and study-abroad programs.

Others are drawn to colleges that are part of a consortium that allows them to share resources and opportunities. The Five College Consortium offers students at Amherst, Smith, Mount Holyoke, Hampshire, and the University of Massachusetts a shared library system, open cross-registration, and transportation between campuses.

While internships are possible for students no matter where they go to school, urban locations often bring more opportunity. Sometimes a particular college is effective in collaborating with local organizations in a way that benefits both the students and the local population. Rhodes College has helped to place student interns at St. Jude Children's Hospital, where they assist with cancer research, and at the Memphis Zoo, where a lucky few are able to work with pandas.

HOW TO RESEARCH COLLEGES

The visit

Nothing brings a college to life like walking the grounds, seeing the people, and catching the vibe. Visitors can go on a student-led campus tour, attend an information session hosted by the admissions office, or look around the campus and public spaces themselves. Watching a game or a performance on campus is a great way to get a sense of student life. If you don't have the funds to travel to faraway campuses, that is understandable. However, if you live fairly close to a college of interest, I encourage you to find the time in your busy schedule to get on campus.

Talk to people

Current students, professors, and staff are great resources, so try to connect with them either on campus or by email. If a student from your high school is now enrolled at a college that you're interested in, ask for a short meeting to discuss her experiences. The admissions office may be able to connect you with one of their student volunteers, with whom you could have a conversation on campus or by phone.

Most high schools have college admissions representatives

visiting their schools almost every day. These representatives offer a short presentation on their college for interested high school students, plus a chance to ask questions and connect with an admissions staff member. Such visits are a great first step in the admissions process. Even if you aren't sure if you would like to attend a particular college, attending several information sessions will give you a sense for how one college is different from others.

Online research

I use many online resources when I research colleges, and I find that the breadth of information available allows a researcher to discover almost anything. A college's own website is a great place to start, and it's helpful to go beyond the admissions pages and read about the academic programs, faculty, student activities, and anything else that sparks your interest. Student publications give you an inside look at the issues and interests of students on campus and can usually be accessed from the main website.

Here are a few more general resources to check out:

Common Data Set is a collaborative effort between data providers in higher education. Most colleges have completed this standard set of questions about their school, and prospective students can review it, gaining insight about admissions, the composition of the student body, and graduation rates. This information is listed on a school's own website. For access, Google "Common Data Set" and the name of a college of interest.

Unigo (www.unigo.com) and **College Prowler (www. collegeprowler.com)** offer reviews and insights from students, along with rankings (everything from "best academics" to "most politically diverse" to "best campus food"), admissions and financial data, and ideas for internships and careers. These sites present information in a teenage-friendly way that makes them top choices for many students.

College Portraits (www.collegeportraits.org) supports transparency in higher education by providing data on public four-year colleges.

College Board (www.collegeboard.org) has a search function that allows students to sift through options to find colleges that match their academic backgrounds and interests.

Naviance (www.naviance.com) is a school-based tool for researching and applying to colleges. If your high school offers Naviance, you can research colleges and see a scattergram chart of how students at your high school have fared in the admissions process.

FREE APPLICATIONS

Applying to college is expensive, with an $11 fee to send SAT scores to each college, plus an application fee that can be as high as $90. Students who apply to more than ten colleges can spend one thousand dollars on application fees alone. However, low-income students who can document their financial need will get fee waivers from many or even all of the colleges that they apply to.

There are also several hundred universities that have no application fee for anyone. Some are selective, while some accept the majority of the students who apply, and they are located throughout the country. The most popular no-application-fee colleges include:

- Baylor
- Beloit
- Carleton
- Case Western
- Colby
- Creighton
- College of Wooster
- Denison
- Florida Southern
- Grinnell
- Hampshire
- Hartwick
- Hobart & William Smith
- Johnson & Wales
- Kenyon
- Lake Forest
- Loyola of Chicago
- Moravian
- Oberlin
- Reed
- Rhodes
- Sewanee
- St. Edward's
- St. Olaf
- Trinity University
- Tulane
- Union College
- Wellesley College

Colleges giving free applications to international students include Bates, Colgate, Gettysburg, and Washington and Lee, among others.

Finding a Financial Fit

For many families, the decision of which college a child will attend is like no other financial decision they have made in their lives. It's almost as if they close their eyes, wait to be told what they will need to pay, and then proceed to beg or borrow in order to cover that amount. Parents who scrutinize the market when buying a house, car, or a piece of furniture may not even attempt to value their child's college education options at all.

"You can't put a price on her future," one of my clients said, while another added that it is nearly impossible to value a college education in dollar terms, because it is so subjective. But while a "return on investment" evaluation is indeed nebulous, it is still important to consider value and the financial fit.

Value and cost considerations are often cast aside in this decision, partly because the college-admissions process is emotionally charged, both for parents and students. Students feel pressure to find their "dream school" and to identify a college that is the perfect fit for them. Parents feel a duty to support their child in this journey, and to provide them with the funds to make their dreams come true. These thoughts and emotions, which are often fueled by college rankings and prestige, lead to college decisions being made because of a "gut feeling." However, if the idea of a "good financial fit" was not addressed, then it's possible that the wrong choice was made.

A second kind of problem can occur when families make a knee-jerk decision about college affordability right from the start. They might decide that they cannot afford college at all, or that they will limit their college search to state colleges before they've even done research on the comparison. While it's true that state universities are often more affordable than private colleges, some private colleges report fewer than 5 percent of their students paying the full sticker price. Many students at many private colleges receive grants that decrease the costs significantly. It is usually worth investigating options beyond the local state college, such as private colleges and community colleges.

Whether you are usually an emotional decision-maker or a rational one, it's important to learn about the financial implications of the college decision.

THE ASTRONOMICAL COST OF COLLEGE

If you are an adult in your forties or fifties, chances are that while your college tuition seemed expensive, it wasn't prohibitive and didn't adversely affect your life. Maybe you worked your way through school, were awarded a meaningful scholarship, or had generous, financially comfortable parents who footed the whole bill, or most of the bill, leaving you with a small amount of loan debt. However you managed it, you emerged from college ready to live independently. Today, fewer and fewer families are able to find a way to pay for college and to come out of the process unscathed.

College tuition costs have risen 1,120 percent over the past 35 years. This is an incredible increase, especially when you consider that food prices increased only 244 percent during this time, and medical care 600 percent. College tuition has risen four times faster than the consumer price index.

INFLATION COMPARISON
Percent Change Since January 1978

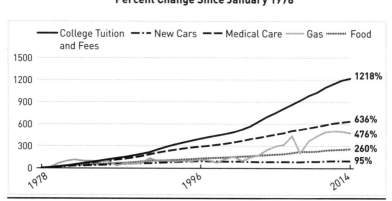

Note: January 1978 is the earlist CPI data for College Tuition and Fees.
Source: Darien Academic Advisors, Bureau of Labor Statistics (Consumer Price Index, September 2014)

Another interesting measure is to compare the cost of tuition to the median US salary. In the 1970s, college tuition at a private university cost just over 50 percent of a typical family's annual income. Today, the cost of a year at a private university is 20 percent *more* than the median income.[103] For example, the median income in 1978 was $13,575, and tuition and room and board at Stanford University was $7,299. A typical family in the United States made significantly more than the Stanford sticker price. But today, the median income is $50,099,[104] and tuition at Stanford and many other private colleges is close to $65,000. So, the typical family in 2014 earns less than the cost of one year at a private college. No wonder the cost of college has parents worried.

A PARENT'S FIRST STEP: DETERMINE WHAT YOU CAN PAY

A financial self-assessment should be the first step in the college planning process. It's helpful to do this before your child falls in love with a college with a $64,000-a-year price tag or decides that he must go to college an expensive plane ride away in California. This assessment asks you to decide how much you are willing and able to pay each year (airfare included) and then explain the assessment to your child. For parents who are used to keeping their child shielded from financial matters, it's time to make the change and involve them in the process.

The financial self-assessment should include all aspects of your family's financial health. It is not enough to simply consider the amount you have saved for college and the amount you can contribute from your current income level.

How much savings do you have, and are you comfortable with this level?

Do you have any debt, and are you in a position to take on more?

What are your current income and income projections for the next five or more years?

How long do you intend to work? Is your retirement savings at a comfortable level, or do you need to increase contributions?

Have you considered all of your children? Decide whether you plan to reserve the same amount for each, or spend different amounts depending on different needs.

Finally, it's important to note that even if you are very well off, you are not required to spend $65,000 a year on your child's college education. Some parents need to see that fact in print to really buy it. So here it is!

These questions are fodder for many long discussions. In a two-parent family, the parents may have different views on the matter. It is highly advisable that you consider these questions at the beginning of the college search, rather than at the end, to decrease the chance that an emotionally charged decision will be made.

Unfortunately, many parents try to avoid the unpleasantness that this can bring and put it off until the time for an admissions decision arrives. The most common reason is that they plan to wait to see what type of scholarships and aid they are offered and then compare them. This is fine for making a final decision (especially because it is tricky to predict what your aid package will be at each individual college), but you should be prepared for this final decision by knowing the maximum tuition amount you are willing and able to spend.

The main pitfall of the wait-and-see strategy is that you might find out that your child has been accepted to wonderful colleges that are outside your financial comfort level. She is elated. Friends, family, and school counselors are congratulating her, and it's difficult to put the brakes on at that point. You may resign yourself to begging and borrowing—hopefully not stealing—to let your child attend.

If the family financial self-assessment was completed at the beginning of the college search process, the college list would have included institutions that are a good "financial fit." A family that has determined that it has $30,000 a year to spend for college and not likely to receive need-based aid would have an entirely different college list than one that decided to look at expenses later. The family who knows what they are willing to pay will be targeting merit scholarships, state universities, and lower-priced private universities. Even families who doubt they can contribute much or any money at all should do a careful financial self-assessment early on.

Now that you have your "number" in mind, it's time to go to the online calculators to determine your EFC and to get an estimate of whether you will qualify for financial aid. The

College Board has an online Net Price Calculator that lets you answer an abbreviated version of the questions you will find on the Free Application for Student Aid (FAFSA). Most colleges offer their own online calculators that estimate what type of institutional aid you can expect to receive at their school. You can find these calculators by doing a Google search with the terms "net price calculator" and the college name. These estimates are helpful because they often include a student contribution amount, either through work study or student loans, and potential merit scholarships.

WHAT TO DO WHEN YOU HAVE NO MONEY FOR COLLEGE

If you have no funds saved for college and nothing to spare from your family budget for college expenses, you are not alone. Millions of students in the United States are in this situation. Low-income students with top grades and test scores have options, but what are the prospects for average students?

Ambitious high school students with average grades and average test results should start by looking at colleges close to home. Rather than taking out extensive loans to cover the tuition, room, and board at a private or state university, they can save money by paying only for courses and books.

When considering local options, students can typically choose from public four-year colleges, for-profit colleges, or community colleges. Most state university systems have branches throughout the state where students can work toward a degree or complete their degree at a low cost in a good-quality program. Community colleges are a wonderful solution because they offer low-cost programs along with academic support that will help a student get through her degree program and be well prepared to transfer to a bachelor's degree program if she so chooses.

Most low-income students meet the requirements for a federal Pell Grant, which awards a maximum of $5,730 a year and does not need to be repaid. This Pell Grant amount covers all or most of the community college tuition, so it's a fantastic option for students who have no savings and little or no funding for college. More than 3.2 million community college students are currently using Pell Grants,[105] and 78 percent of them work part-time while they go to school. After they finish their two years in a community college program, they can transfer to a four-year program. The average public four-year college's yearly tuition is $8,893, so a student who uses a Pell Grant will have only a small amount to cover with his own earnings.

The least favorable option among these choices is the for-profit college. They average $15,130 a year in tuition and market themselves to low-income and minority students. Over 90 percent of for-profit college graduates have taken out loans, and the average debt at graduation is $40,000. Unfortunately, only 32 percent of for-profit college students graduate within six years, so many are left with extensive debt and no degree.[106]

If you are a strong student without financial means, you may be eligible for merit aid and need-based aid at many colleges. To qualify for most awards, it's important that you have high test results to go along with your good grades. You are encouraged to apply widely, use application-fee waivers to reduce the costs of applying, and to complete the FAFSA (the financial aid request form). Good students can also consider tuition-free colleges such as the US service academies, Webb Institute, Deep

Springs College, or the Macaulay Honors College at City University of New York. Talented musicians can consider tuition-free Curtis Institute of Music, and those willing to work during their college years can consider College of the Ozarks or Berea College, both tuition-free.

FINANCIAL AID: HOW DOES IT REALLY WORK?

There are a few things that almost everyone knows about financial aid: a family's income and financial situation will be reviewed, and this will affect the amount of help that they get in paying for college. This help involves grants and loans, in some undetermined ratio. There is involvement from the colleges, the government, and private lenders. But beyond this, there is a lot of uncertainty, and even those of us who understand the steps in the process do not always understand the big picture.

In order to apply for federal financial aid, parents complete the FAFSA, a Department of Education form, which asks a variety of questions about your financial situation and your child's earnings and savings. The family is given an Expected Family Contribution (EFC), which is the minimum amount they are expected to pay for college each year. The EFC is calculated according to a formula established by Congress. This formula is enacted by the Department of Education, not by individual colleges. Your family's taxed and untaxed income, assets, and benefits (such as unemployment or Social Security) are all considered in the formula. Also considered are your family size and the number of family members who will attend college. The calculation does not consider retirement funds, but it does look at savings, and some colleges ask for a supplemental form so that they may consider home equity.[107]

When your student applies to colleges, each institution will give him a financial aid package based on that EFC. Their goal is to cover the amount beyond the EFC, called the "demonstrated need," by offering grants or suggesting loans. It sounds fair enough, and many parents are optimistic that it will all work out for their student.

The first pitfall is the EFC itself. It is a calculation that leaves some families wondering if there has been a mistake. The amount that they are asked to pay seems to be much higher than a rational person would determine is possible. I worked with a family of four with a $100,000 income and modest savings, which was given an EFC of $18,000 a year. This family that takes home $6,000 a month is suddenly expected to pay $1,500 monthly toward college? Families making $185,000 a year may be surprised to find out that they don't qualify for any aid whatsoever and could be expected to pay over one-third of their take-home salary toward tuition. Parents who were expecting the EFC to be a fair assessment of their ability to pay find this to be the first sign of bad things to come.

But then they remember the phrase "we meet demonstrated need" that they have heard at college visits and fairs. A college that meets demonstrated need promises that they will fund all of your tuition beyond the EFC. They are essentially saying, "You pay the EFC that was calculated for you, and we'll pay the rest." As parents look at the astronomical college-tuition price tags, they remember this promise and think that surely something fair can be worked out. Even though the EFC calculation seems to ask too much of them, if the colleges will cover the balance, they might be able to swing it.

There is a general perception that many colleges guarantee to meet the full demonstrated need of all accepted students. But only sixty-one universities out of more than 2,700 in the United States actually claim to meet the full demonstrated need.[108] They include very few state universities and are mostly elite institutions with low acceptance rates. So the EFC, which is far higher than we could possibly pay in the first place, is not even the bottom line. Are parents expected to fill the demonstrated-need void by digging into savings, or through an assortment of loans and scholarships?

Mysteries of merit aid uncovered

Parents who are disappointed with their EFC and the small number of colleges that meet demonstrated need turn their hopes and thoughts to merit scholarships. These scholarships do not consider financial need, but are awarded on the basis of academic, athletic, or artistic merit, or in a few unique situations and special-interest cases.

I get more questions about merit scholarships from my students than about almost any other topic. Are there really scholarships for left-handed people, golf caddies, and vegetarians? Do you need to have all As to get a merit scholarship? There are indeed scholarships for people with unique personal characteristics or interests, and they do not always require top grades in school. But it's important to note that most merit scholarships are awarded by colleges during the admissions process and do not require searching the Internet or thumbing through scholarship directories (though some are available through these sources).

There is over $13 billion in merit aid available each year, with $11 billion awarded by the colleges themselves and $2 billion from state governments.[109] The amount available from private scholarship sources is much smaller, both in number of scholarships awarded and in the size of the awards. Students winning merit scholarships from outside sources are required to report them to their college financial aid offices. These funds are counted as a resource and may reduce the size of the grant portion of the financial aid package.

Institutional aid

The largest chunk of scholarship money available comes from the colleges, and in most cases, you are automatically considered when you apply for admission. Yes, there really is a scholarship for lefties: it is awarded by Juniata College, through the Frederick and Mark F. Buckley program. This award is for $1,000 to $1,500 and goes to selected left-handed students with top grades who are admitted to Juniata.

Most colleges award some form of merit scholarship, and your best chance of getting one is to be in the top 10 percent of their applicant pool. Colleges use the merit scholarship money to attract students who might not otherwise attend their school. If you are a top student with the credentials to get into an Ivy League college, you might get a merit award as large as $20,000 a year from the University of Miami, Tulane, Emory, or any of hundreds of other colleges. If you are a student who would be admitted to Tulane or Emory, but you are not in the top of their applicant pool, they won't offer you a scholarship—but a less selective college might do so.

There are a few dozen ultra-selective colleges, including the Ivy League colleges, Tufts, and Amherst, that do not award any merit scholarships, reserving all of the funding for their need-based financial aid programs. Still others, such as Stanford and Georgetown, award athletic scholarships without regard to need, but no other merit scholarships, reserving the rest for students with need. However, the number of colleges that do not offer merit scholarships is small, so most students will apply to colleges that consider them for these awards.

If you would like to earn a merit scholarship, you should choose your application list carefully. Consider applying to colleges where your academic profile is toward the top of the accepted student range, and research scholarships online at sites such as www.meritaid.com. This site allows you to search by college to review available scholarships, or to enter your profile and get a list of colleges that are likely to offer you merit aid.

Athletic scholarships

An athletic scholarship is the dream of many young athletes, and also a dream for the parents who financially funded and supported their child's sports career. The most important things that I have learned about sports scholarships are that they are very difficult to get, and that when you do get one, it is often not what you expected.

According to data from the NCAA, scholarships are given to just 2 percent of the 6.4 million high school athletes in the United States. Even if you are the best athlete in your high school, your league, or your state, you still might not be in the top 2 percent in the country.

The other big surprise is that athletic scholarships are typically rather small. The average amount of an athletic scholarship is less than $11,000 per year, with many students only winning $2,000 a year despite being highly recruited athletes. Full scholarships are more common for revenue-driving sports such as football and men's and women's basketball. Women can also get full scholarships in gymnastics, volleyball, and tennis.

If you were nationally ranked in your sport, you may still go on to become a college athlete, but with no scholarship. Sixty percent of college athletes receive no athletic scholarship aid whatsoever. Many but not all of these athletes attend Division III or Ivy League colleges that do not offer sports scholarships.

Scholarships for minority, low-income, and first-generation college students

The majority of low-income, high-achieving students do not apply to any selective colleges, thus forgoing the generous grant aid that could have been available to them. A report by the Century Foundation found that only 44 percent of low-income high school seniors with high standardized test scores enroll in a four-year college at all, and that most of them attend local schools.[110] These students were not likely to know people who could advise them about college and financial aid opportunities, and they may not have had the funds for college application fees.

The landscape is beginning to change. Non-profits and scholarship programs have been effective at getting low-income students to consider college, including at campuses away from home that have higher graduation rates and better aid opportunities. The dominant player is Questbridge, a non-profit that identifies and prepares low-income students, and then matches them with opportunities at one of its thirty-five partner colleges. Questbridge students have received over $2 billion in full scholarships from the partner colleges. The students are a big presence on campuses, with almost three hundred undergraduates at Stanford this year, which is 4 percent of the student body. At Amherst, 11 percent of the student body is from Questbridge, and at Pomona it's 9 percent.[111]

Others include the Dell Scholars Program, which awards grants to three hundred new low-income students each year, also providing mentoring, support, technology, and a networking community. The Gates Millennium Scholars Program awards one thousand scholarships to low-income students of color who plan to major in a STEM field. Academically oriented young people who come from low-income families should not be deterred from applying to college, and they should look to these and other resources for help along the way.

State aid

Several years ago, thirteen states had the fantastic idea of using lottery proceeds to support high school students and encourage them to attend college in their home state. The most well-known program is the Georgia HOPE scholarship, which is available to all Georgia students who maintain a 3.0 GPA in rigorous courses. These students are eligible for about $4,000 a year in free grant money if they attend a college within the state of Georgia. The program does not consider financial need, as it offers only merit scholarships.

Many of the states eliminated their state aid programs when the economy declined in 2009, also citing concerns that aid was going to students without significant need. But today there is still $2 billion in aid coming from the states each year. Still going strong with merit scholarships are the Florida Bright Futures program, Arkansas Academic Challenge program, Alaska Scholars Award, Louisiana Tuition Opportunity Program, Mississippi Eminent Scholars Program, South Carolina Palmetto Scholarship program, New Mexico Lottery Success Scholarship, Nevada Millennium Scholarship, and West Virginia Promise program. Residents of these states can earn up to $5,000 a year by enrolling in colleges within their home state.

National Merit Scholarship Program

The National Merit Scholarship Program is an academic recognition and scholarship program which has been around since 1955. All juniors who take the PSAT (more than 1.5 million students in 2013) are considered for a National Merit Scholarship. The program names sixteen thousand semifinalists who have the highest PSAT results in their state (so those who live in states with higher average scores need to perform better than they would in states with lower average scores). Through further evaluation, they are narrowed to eight thousand finalists. The finalists each receive a single $2,500 scholarship payment from the National Merit Scholarship Program, and they are eligible for larger funds given by corporations or colleges.

Many National Merit Finalists enroll at elite colleges, but plenty of them enroll at colleges that offer generous scholarship and benefit packages. The University of Oklahoma has more National Merit Finalists than any other public university because of its commitment to attracting and retaining these scholars. The school has enrolled more than seven hundred National Merit Finalists who are enjoying a free ride to college. Full scholarships are also offered to Finalists at Baylor and the Universities of Alabama, Delaware, Houston, and Richmond, among others.

Private organizations

Unfortunately, there are not as many merit scholarships offered by private organizations as many people think, or hope, there are. The larger scholarship award programs include the Coca-Cola Foundation, which offers a top prize of $20,000 to fifty lucky students who are evaluated on their academic and extracurricular profiles, but not on their financial need status; the Davidson Fellows, which awards $50,000 scholarships to students who have completed a significant piece of work; and the Buick Achievers Scholarship, which is a renewable scholarship of $25,000 for students interested in automobiles and majoring in engineering, design, or business.

Students often have success looking for merit scholarships within their own communities. Although they are often small in size, these scholarships can be helpful. Consider local organizations such as Rotary, Kiwanis, Elks, Junior League, a women's club, or your town Chamber of Commerce. Sports organizations such as the local Little League or soccer association might offer awards for past players. Your high school guidance counselor is probably knowledgeable about local merit award opportunities.

If you have an unusual major or career field in mind, you may qualify for a merit scholarship from a professional association in this field. You can also look at www.meritaid.com or www.fastweb.com for additional resources for merit aid.

As you seek merit scholarships, it is also important to keep it in perspective. Meaningful awards are not common, and full scholarships are extremely rare. Mark Kantrowitz, publisher of Edvisors.com, did a large, statistically significant study of more than 950,000 bachelor-degree candidates and found that less than 1 percent of students got enough grant money to get a free ride to college. He found that only one in eight got any type of scholarship or free money toward college whatsoever.[112]

COMMUNITY COLLEGE TO BACHELOR'S DEGREE

One of the most cost-effective ways to get a bachelor's degree is to attend community college for two years and then transfer to a four-year university. The average cost of a full course load at a community college is only $3,264 per year. It is possible to earn two years of college credits for less than seven thousand dollars![113]

Students who plan to transfer to a state or private university need to plan ahead and be sure to select classes that are transferable to their university and intended major. For those who worry about missing out on student-life opportunities, there are more than one hundred US community colleges that have residence halls and meal plans, and most offer sports, extracurricular activities, and campus events.

FACTS ABOUT STUDENT LOAN DEBT IN THE UNITED STATES

TOTAL AMOUNT OF STUDENT LOAN DEBT IN THE USA	$1.1 TRILLION
Average student loan balance in 1993	$15,073
Average student loan balance in 2014	$27,547
Borrowers who owe more than $50,000	10%
Borrowers who owe more than $100,000	3%
Percent increase in student-loan borrowers, 2007–2012	31%

Source: Malcolm Hadley. "Millennials' ball-and-chain: Student loan debt." *USA Today*, July 1, 2013.http://www.usatoday.com/story/money/personalfinance/2013/06/30/student-loan-debt-economic-effects/2388189/

THINGS TO KNOW ABOUT STUDENT LOANS

Today, students are often turning to loans to cover college tuition costs. This path, however, comes with many strings attached. It has been shown that young adults with excessive debt are risk-averse and less likely to buy or rent a home, afford a car payment, start a business, get married, have children, or otherwise move forward in their lives.[114] The Gallup/Purdue survey that we discussed on page 24 found that only 2 percent of young adults with $20,000 to $40,000 in debt rated themselves as "thriving."[115]

The decision about student loans is the first major financial decision that many young people will make. Here is some important information for prospective college students to consider: if you are like most high school students, you've given very little thought to the magnitude and logistics of college financing and what it really means for you and your family. Your reference points are limited, and you may not fully understand how loans work, what typical entry-level job salaries are like, or how your parents would have to adjust their lifestyles in order to accommodate high college-tuition payments.

You might accept the idea of taking out student loans without understanding exactly how that will affect your life in the future. Student loans can empower you to get an education that can lead to success, but it's important to understand what a reasonable debt level is, and to evaluate funding options to be sure that you can manage your loans.

If you are considering student loans, it is crucial that you start with any federal loans that you are eligible for, before taking out loans from private lenders. Even children from wealthy families who do not qualify for financial aid will still be allowed to take out an unsubsidized Stafford loan. This means that they are eligible for a Stafford loan with an interest rate of 3.86 percent in 2014, instead of rates as high as 9 or 10 percent offered by private lenders. You must file the FAFSA in order to qualify for the Stafford loan. Many families who know that they won't qualify for aid but do plan to take out loans miss out on the low Stafford rates because they do not file the FAFSA. Students taking the Stafford loan have this lower rate, and they have some protection if they are unemployed, but they are limited to borrowing $5,500 the first year, $6,500 the second year, and $7,500 in subsequent years.

Now that you know about this basic fact about student loans, let's look at a typical scenario that you might consider.

Let's say you are considering two college choices. After your parents have paid their agreed-upon amount, you are left to fund either $5,000 a year at College A or $15,000 a year at College B. College B costs only $10,000 per year more, and that doesn't sound like a big difference to you.

Because you filed for the FAFSA, you are eligible for an unsubsidized Stafford loan of $5,500, at a rate of 3.86 percent. If you choose College A, you take a $5,000 loan each year. You do not have to start paying off this loan until you graduate, but interest starts accumulating as soon as the loan is drawn. At graduation, your total debt will be approximately $21,800.

If you choose College B, you will take a $5,500 Stafford loan the first year, at 3.86 percent, but also a $9,500 loan from a private lender who charges approximately 9 percent. Due to interest accruals, at the end of year one, you have $16,100 in debt. You will continue to take the maximum that you can from the Stafford loan over the next three years and to cover the rest with the more expensive private loans. At graduation, your total debt will be $69,900—far more than you may have expected, given that the cost to attend College B is "only" $10,000 per year more than College A per year.

Now, take a moment to think about what your life will be like at the age of twenty-three. You will have graduated from college, and hopefully you will have a job in your intended field. Do you know what typical starting salaries are? Salary examples on the high end are those of engineers and software developers, who could make $60,000 a year right out of college, and investment bankers or consultants, who could make over $100,000 including their bonuses. On the lower end, a job in public relations might pay only $30,000, and if you are among the many college graduates who are able to land only minimum-wage, part-time, or unpaid positions in the still-tough economic climate, you'll be making considerably less. Do you plan to have a car, a smartphone, or your own apartment? Do you hope to save for a down-payment on your own home? You will make monthly payments for these lifestyle choices, but you will still have your student-loan debt with you.

For example, if you chose College A and have a standard

Stafford repayment plan offering a ten-year loan term, you will be paying $219 a month. If you chose College B, with a ten-year loan term for your private loan as well, your monthly loan payments will be $810.

Let's say you got that engineering job paying $60,000 a year and your monthly take-home salary after taxes is about $3,500. If you chose College A, the monthly loan payment would be quite reasonable. Even if you chose College B and have to pay $810 a month, it would be expensive but still possible with your high income. However, if you have the lower-paying job in public relations, your take-home pay is only $2,000 per month. If you are burdened with an $810-a-month loan payment every month for the next ten years, it will be difficult to live independently and meet other financial goals in your life.

It is important to understand that when you take out a loan, you are paying more for college than students who did not take out a loan are paying. In ten years, after you have paid off your loan to College A, you will have paid $4,500 in interest expense. If you chose College B, you will have paid $27,200 in interest alone! If you are unable to make payments and default on your loan, interest will accumulate and your debt will grow and grow.

While the example above may seem simple and obvious to adults who have been dealing with mortgages, car payments, or credit-card bills for years, it can be eye-opening to a teenager.

A recent Wells Fargo survey of 1,141 young adults between the ages of twenty-two and thirty-two found that half of the responders had financed part of their education with student loans. Fifty-two percent said that their debt was "their biggest financial concern" and 42 percent found their debt "overwhelming." These students wished that they had known more about financial planning, with 79 percent of them responding that basic personal finance should be taught in high school. The topic of "how loans work" was identified as one of their top three interests.[116]

A CRAZY THOUGHT: LET'S SCRAP THE LOANS AND MAKE STATE COLLEGES FREE

Many countries in Europe have long offered free or very low-cost university tuition to their students. In Germany, for the first time in history, the government recently instituted yearly university tuition fees of only one thousand euros (a paltry sum by US standards). Students protested en masse and collected more than seventy thousand signatures disputing this tuition. The students won, and tuition is free again. It makes me wonder why more American students don't protest to try to get state universities to be fully funded by the government. Oh, what's that you say? The U.S. Department of Education doesn't have enough money to fund the state universities? Actually it does, and then some.

Federal Student Aid, a part of the U.S. Department of Education that administers the FAFSA, has 1,200 employees and is the largest provider of student loans in the United States. It provides more than $150 billion in federal loans, grants, and work-study funds each year according to its own website. Jordan Weissmann did a fascinating and provocative study in the *Atlantic Monthly* showing how the federal government could make public college tuition-free without spending a penny more on education. Public universities collected $62.6 billion in tuition from students in 2012. The federal government spent $69 billion in 2013 on grants, tax breaks, and work-study funding alone, according to the New America Foundation. This does not include the $107 billion that the federal government spent on loans.

What if the federal government used that $69 billion to fully fund state universities? Weissmann wrote, "If we were scrapping our current system and starting from scratch, Washington could make public college tuition free with the money it sets aside in scattershot attempts to make college affordable today."[117]

A new government policy like this would be good for the 76 percent of American students who attend public colleges. But it would be bad for students at private colleges, who would have benefits cut. Particularly loud opposition could come from the for-profit colleges, which currently receive 25 percent of the federal aid, despite educating only 10 percent of the students and having a 50-percent loan-default rate. Still, it may be a trade worth considering.

COLLEGE TUITION AS A FINANCIAL INVESTMENT

Although we think of college as an educational experience and a time for personal growth, it is also a financial investment. We need to step back and look at the $100,000 or $250,000 that is going toward college and ask ourselves, What is the payback? Will my child have a better future if she has a $250,000 degree, or will it be roughly the same no matter what we pay?

Without a crystal ball, we will never know for sure. But these questions are important to consider because they move the conversation about college to a focus on outcomes and value. PayScale, a Seattle-based company that tracks wages, recently organized its data by college to produce a "College

Education ROI [Return on Investment] Ranking."[118] PayScale uses salary data to rank colleges based on their total cost and alumni earnings. You can view the twenty-year ROI, or sort the colleges by major and location, and consider the tuition data with or without financial-aid costs.

PAYSCALE TOP 10 COLLEGES RANKED BY TWENTY-YEAR NET RETURN ON INVESTMENT (ROI)

RANK	SCHOOL NAME	2013 COST	20 YEAR NET ROI	ANNUAL ROI	GRAD RATE
1	Harvey Mudd College	$229,500	$980,900	8.8%	88%
2	California Institute of Technology (Caltech)	$220,400	$837,600	8.3%	92%
3	Massachusetts Institute of Technology (MIT)	$223,400	$831,100	8.2%	93%
4	Stanford University	$236,300	$789,500	7.8%	95%
5	Colorado School of Mines (In-State)	$114,200	$783,400	11.0%	67%
6	Georgia Institute of Technology (In-State)	$92,250	$755,600	11.9%	79%
7	Rose-Hulman Institute of Technology (RHIT)	$217,400	$736,200	7.8%	76%
8	Polytechnic Institute of New York University (NYU-Poly)	$223,900	$724,500	7.7%	62%
9	Stevens Institute of Technology	$250,900	$722,400	7.2%	78%
10	Colorado School of Mines (Out-Of-State)	$178,500	$719,000	8.6%	67%

Source: PayScale, "2014 PayScale College ROI Report," accessed October 14, 2014, http://www.payscale.com/college-roi/.

The winners in the PayScale rankings are the engineering schools, and it often surprises people to see colleges that they have never heard of in the top ten. Besides serving as another resource with which to shatter the myth that only elite-college graduates are successful, PayScale has also been successful in getting students to look at value and factor their future career earnings into their college decisions.

But the PayScale study is not a perfect analysis. The data is self-reported by people who visit the site, and although there are a lot of data points, they are not verified and do not include alumni who are out of the workforce. The data also excludes alumni who have graduate degrees. Even if the PayScale study was completely accurate, an ROI ranking only includes one facet of the college admissions decision. It studies what other people earned, but it doesn't tell a person about his own potential earnings. Every person has the ability to develop his Success Profile and have a great career no matter what college he attends.

Your child's future career goals and projected earnings are an important part of the financial-fit analysis. But this decision has to go hand in hand with a general evaluation of colleges. Perhaps you determine that a state university is the right financial choice, but you worry about your son succeeding in large classes. You might be concerned about paying extra for a liberal-arts college, but you know that your daughter will thrive with the increased faculty interaction and getting to know classmates from all over the world.

The financial fit is an important metric in the college admissions process. For some families, it will be the only factor considered, and for others, it will be one of many things considered in selecting a college. But for all, it's something to be considered at the onset of the process.

CASE STUDIES IN FINANCIAL-AID DECISION-MAKING

The following case studies show how some families tested the value of college and considered the potential returns on their investments. The examples are based on true stories and realistic estimates of financial aid and merit awards. The SAT scores include only the critical-reading and math sections, and not the writing section, since it is being eliminated by the College Board and was not consistently used in admissions decisions prior to its elimination.

CASE 1

JULIANNE

Julianne is from Fairfield, Connecticut, and hopes to attend a college with a strong liberal-arts program and great student life. She isn't sure what she wants to major in, but she's thinking about law school in the future. She wants to attend college within a three-hour drive of her home, and she applied strategically to include colleges where she might get merit scholarships.

The Stats: Julianne is ranked 10th in her class, and she has a GPA close to 4.0 with very high standardized testing of 720 in math and 740 in critical reading. She is active at her high school: she plays two sports, does volunteer work, and writes for the school newspaper.

Family Finances: Julianne's dad is school administrator making $72,000 a year, and her mom is a part-time preschool teacher making $13,000 a year. They have two children, a small amount of equity in their home, and $87,000 in savings, in addition to their retirement accounts, which are not included in the financial-aid equation. Julianne's parents worry about how they will fund college for Julianne as well as for her younger brother, who is not a top student, and have decided that they have $7,000 per year to pay for Julianne's college.

The Offers: At the University of Connecticut (UConn), Julianne is eligible for in-state tuition, which is $30,000.* She gets a $7,000 grant from UConn, leaving a balance of $23,000. Julianne can take out a Stafford loan for the maximum amount, and her parents would raise their contribution to $10,000 a year, taking a parent PLUS loan for the balance. The total debt at graduation would be $29,300 for Julianne and $29,100 for her parents.

At Roger Williams, a private university in Rhode Island, the tuition is $52,000. Julianne is in the top 20 percent of the applicant pool and would receive an $18,000 grant based both on need and merit. This leaves $34,000 to cover with loans and payments. Because this is so much higher than UConn, Roger Williams is eliminated as an option.

At Trinity College, a top liberal arts college in Hartford, the tuition is $61,000. Julianne is offered a $52,000 grant, based on financial need. Julianne's parents can pay $7,000 a year, leaving Julianne with only $2,000 a year to finance herself. She can do work study and take out a $2,000 annual Stafford loan. She would graduate with $8,700 in debt.

The Decision: Julianne chose to enroll at Trinity College. She was able to get this great deal at Trinity because it is a well-funded liberal-arts college with a commitment to financial aid for middle-income families. However, the admissions profile of accepted students is very high. Students who did not have Julianne's high GPA and test scores would not have this option.

---

* Throughout the case studies, the tuition amounts listed include room and board and all other costs to attend, including transportation, which varies for each person.

CASE 2

JOAQUIN

Joaquin is a New Jersey resident who loves the ocean and hopes to have a career in oceanography or marine mammal biology. His first choice is the University of Miami because of its strong marine science program and its location near both the ocean and a multicultural city. He is also applying to Rutgers and the University of Tampa, which have good marine science programs.

The Stats: Joaquin has a 3.7 GPA and SAT scores of 680 in math and 640 in critical reading. He plays two varsity sports and works at a sleepaway camp each summer.

Family Finances: Joaquin's mom stays at home and his dad makes $220,000 as a financial analyst. They have $400,000 in savings and retirement funds and $40,000 in a 529 college savings fund. They are well-off but are hoping to qualify for financial aid or merit scholarships. Joaquin's dad is worried about the longevity of his job in finance, as well as funding college for Joaquin's two younger siblings. They have decided that $35,000 a year is the amount they are willing to pay for college.

The Offers: At University of Miami, tuition is $61,000 a year and Joaquin would receive no financial aid or scholarships. Joaquin realizes that the costs are almost double the amount that his parents had agreed to pay. He is willing to take loans and work part-time, and he hopes his parents will consider increasing the amount of their contribution.

At Rutgers, the in-state tuition is $27,000 and Joaquin would receive no financial aid.

At the University of Tampa, the tuition is $35,000 and Joaquin is awarded at $12,000 merit scholarship, making the total cost $23,000 a year.

The Decision: Joaquin and his parents decide on the University of Miami, after several weeks of heated discussion. They realize that Rutgers and the University of Tampa are better financial fits, and that both offer excellent academic programs. However, Joaquin prefers the academic program and campus life of University of Miami and was determined to attend. They decided to allocate $10,000 of Joaquin's 529 college savings plan to each year, leaving a yearly tuition balance of $51,000. After subtracting his parents' $35,000 payment, Joaquin is left with a $16,000 balance. He agrees to take out the maximum Stafford loan amount and private loans to cover this amount.

At graduation, Joaquin has nearly $75,000 in debt. He is able to get a job as an oceanographer, paying $50,000, so he is able to pay his $870 monthly loan payment, but money is tight. Joaquin's parents are glad that they stuck to the contribution level that they agreed upon at the beginning of the college search process. Joaquin's father was laid off from his financial-analyst position and spent a year without a job before finding new employment at a lower salary.

CASE 3

CAROLINE

Caroline lives in Vero Beach, Florida, but is drawn to the vibrancy of city life and hopes to attend college in the Northeast. She fell in love with Boston University (BU). Caroline plans to work in a museum and is looking for a college where she can have internship opportunities.

The Stats: Caroline has a 3.6 GPA student with SAT scores of 600 in math and 640 in critical reading, and she is active in the arts and volunteer work. Her academic profile is at the lower end of BU's range, but she hopes to be admitted.

Family Finances: Caroline's father is a consultant, with an income of $110,000, and her mother makes $55,000 as the director of a non-profit. They have savings of $350,000, which means that they are unlikely to qualify for any institutional aid. They determine that they have $20,000 per year for Caroline's college tuition.

The Offers: At Boston University, which costs $60,000 a year, Caroline is accepted and offered a $1,500 merit scholarship. This is reflective of the fact that she was not at the top of their applicant pool. Caroline and her family are faced with costs of $38,500 a year over their comfort zone. The aid package comes with specific loan suggestions that would make it all possible. Caroline could take a $5,500 Stafford loan and another $10,000 in private student loans. Her parents can take out $23,000 in parent PLUS loans. Total debt at graduation would be $71,000 for Caroline and close to $100,000 for her parents.

Caroline also applied to Saint Joseph's University in Philadelphia, which has all the benefits of big-city life, but also a grassy campus and a close community of students. Saint Joseph's University costs $53,000 a year. Because Caroline's grades and testing are at the higher end of their admissions range, she is offered a $15,000 merit grant and a $7,400 need-based grant. The family's annual cost would be only $30,600.

The Decision: The family is faced with weighing Saint Joseph's against Boston University. They consider rankings, facilities, academic programs, student life, general reputation, and internship opportunities. They decide that Saint Joseph's is a better value and BU is not worth the extensive debt. Caroline takes the Stafford loan maximum and her parents take a PLUS loan for the small balance. Caroline enrolls at Saint Joseph's, and she secures an internship at the prestigious Barnes Foundation in her second year.

NICHOLAS

Nicholas is the valedictorian of a public high school in North Carolina, and he wants to be a writer or a doctor. He is impressed with the top-tier colleges that he has visited and hopes to attend any Ivy League college.

The Stats: Nicholas is first in his class with SAT scores of 780 in math and 800 in critical reading. He is a published writer who has also won several state- and national-level science awards.

Family Finances: Nicholas's father is a doctor and his mother is a nurse. They have a high income: $350,000 in the past year. However, his father is concerned that changes in the medical field could decrease his income in the future. He is also concerned that they have only $150,000 in savings, considerably lower than they had hoped because of the high cost of his own medical school and college loans.

The Offers: Nicholas is accepted at Yale, Brown, and Columbia, where the tuition is over $60,000 a year, and he would receive no aid or scholarships at any of the schools.

At the University of North Carolina at Chapel Hill, where he is a top applicant, Nicholas is awarded the prestigious Morehead-Cain Scholarship, which includes free tuition, fees, and books, plus a summer travel program.

The Decision: Nicholas and his parents are surprised at how easy it is to turn down three Ivy League colleges. The Morehead-Cain scholarship is an amazing opportunity, and UNC offers everything that Nicholas was looking for.

ROBERTO

Roberto is the valedictorian of his high school in East Los Angeles. He is fascinated by technology, computers, and math. Roberto doesn't know many people who have gone away to college and doesn't know if his family could afford anything other than the local options.

The Stats: Roberto has a 4.0 GPA, a 580 critical-reading SAT score, and a 740 math SAT score.

Family Finances: Roberto's mother cleans houses and his father works in the kitchen of a local restaurant. Roberto works part-time at Radio Shack. The family has no savings and no means to pay for college.

The Offers: Roberto's teacher recommended him for Questbridge, a program that matches high-achieving, low-income students with colleges. Through Questbridge, Roberto is accepted to the University of Chicago with a full scholarship including expenses. His other option is a community college paid for with a Pell Grant, and a part-time job to cover books and expenses.

The Decision: Roberto enrolls at the University of Chicago, majors in computer science, and gets an internship in software design.

CASE 6

EVELYN

Evelyn is an ambitious student from Arkansas who knows what she is looking for in a college. She wants to go to college out of state, preferably in Texas, since it isn't too far from home. She does not want to go to a large state university, preferring smaller classes and a closer sense of community. She wants to be in a vibrant city.

The Stats: Evelyn is a B+ student with SAT scores of 620 in math and 640 in critical reading. She plays three sports and is very involved at her high school.

Family Finances: Evelyn's father is a lawyer in private practice, and her mother is a public defender. They have a current income of $145,000. In the past, Evelyn's father had a higher- paying job, and he was able to save $400,000 and build up nearly a half-million dollars in home equity. Because of this, they will not be eligible for need-based financial aid, but Evelyn's parents are still concerned about the high cost of college. They would like to pay no more than $35,000 a year, but they realize that this might not be possible if Evelyn goes out of state.

The Offers: At Southern Methodist University (SMU) in Dallas, the tuition and fees are $64,000 a year. Evelyn does not qualify for any financial aid or merit scholarships because she is not in the top of SMU's applicant pool, and her parents' savings and home equity exclude the possibility of need-based financial aid.

At St. Edward's University in Austin, the tuition and fees are $51,000 per year. Evelyn is offered a $15,000 annual merit scholarship, resulting in a total cost of $36,000.

At the University of Arkansas, in-state tuition, room, and board total only $18,000. Evelyn is eligible for the Arkansas Academic Scholarship of $2,000, making the total cost just $16,000 per year.

The Decision: Evelyn chose St. Edward's, and she is excited

QUESTION 12:
A high school student secures a college loan for $80,000 at 8 percent interest. Assuming the economy is still in the tank after graduation, that only low-paying service-sector jobs are available and factoring for inflation, can the loan be repaid before the student dies of old age?

Show your work on the bottom of the page.

THESE NEW SAT QUESTIONS ARE A LITTLE TOO "RELEVANT."

JOHN COLE

about going to college in the thriving city of Austin at a college known for its diverse population and strong academic program. Although the University of Arkansas was a better value, Evelyn wanted a college experience that involved going out of state, living in a city, and being part of a small campus community. Her parents will pay $31,000 a year from savings, and Evelyn will take out a Stafford loan of $5000 per year.

RESOURCES

One great source for college financial information is the US Department of Education's College Affordability and Transparency Center, http://collegecost.ed.gov. There you will find the College Scorecard and the College Navigator, which will help you learn about the affordability and value of colleges that interest you. The *Chronicle of Education* has another interesting site focused on the theme of education as an investment, funded by the Gates Foundation, at collegerealitycheck.com.

Families who want to delve more deeply into advanced funding strategies should consider working with an expert in this area. Certain independent educational consultants who are professional members of the Independent Educational Consultants Association (IECA) have expertise in identifying the right colleges for your child by evaluating how your Expected Family Contribution (EFC) plays out at various colleges. They are able to create a college list that is affordable for parents. You can find an IECA-member consultant in your area by going to www.iecaonline.com. C. Claire Law is one consultant with expertise in financial aid who works with families throughout the United States. Although it may seem contradictory to pay a professional for help with financial aid, the end result may help you to save money.

ARE PRIVATE HIGH SCHOOLS WORTH THE MONEY?

With private-school tuition at astronomically high levels, many parents who might previously have sent their children to private schools are now questioning whether it is worth spending so much money that could be used for college. There are day schools in the New York and Boston areas that cost over $40,000 per year and boarding schools with tuition nearing $58,000. Parents can potentially spend over a half-million dollars before their child even starts college.

There are some examples in which private schools have been life-changing for a child and worth every penny. I have known students with learning issues who finally found their groove and came to believe in themselves after attending an independent school with learning support. I have worked with students whose public schools were lacking, and who were inspired and challenged at private schools. Also, students who experience bullying may benefit from the fresh start at a new school.

But if you live in an area with good public schools and you do not have unlimited funds, you have to evaluate whether there is any long-term value in sending your child to private school. If your primary reason for considering independent schools is because of the school's college-placement list or your belief that they will give your child a better chance at getting into a top college, think again. Keep in mind that elite colleges

Sidebar Continues

now turn over every rock trying to find good candidates. They visit thousands of high schools each year to recruit students and to spread the word about their colleges. A simple check of admissions statistics will tell you that all of the top colleges have more students from public schools than from private schools. The days of feeder schools and special connections with top colleges are over. Plus, as we've learned again and again, getting into a top college is not in itself a golden ticket.

College in the Future

So far, this book's advice has taken the current state of higher education, especially as it exists in the United States, as a given. However, the concept of the American university as we know it is nearing a tipping point. We can't go on much longer with high tuition, unfathomable student-debt levels, and poor results from the academic experience itself. Online education and new ideas about learning and evaluation have entered the market, challenging the old model. Higher education is on the cusp of massive and lasting change, which will be driven by technology. Just like the newspaper and music industries, higher education will be forced to weather the change and adapt.

We don't know exactly what the future of education will look like. However, it is likely that we'll look back in a decade or two and recall with wonder the vast changes that have occurred. Hopefully, we will see more affordable, credible alternatives that better prepare students for the job market. Current high school students may eventually find themselves competing for jobs with people whose education took a very different path from theirs. That said, even current students can draw on some of the new developments that this chapter will explore. Doing so is an excellent way to develop their Success Profiles outside the traditional confines of high school and college.

ONLINE EDUCATION REVOLUTION

If you remember the first online classes, you probably wouldn't think that they would be a precursor to a trend that will revolutionize higher education. These classes were thought to be poor-quality substitutes for real college classes, an option only for students who had no other choice.

Fast-forward to today, when there are more than six million people enrolled in online college courses, representing 31 percent of all college students.[119] Not only for-profit colleges like the University of Phoenix (which has 250,000 undergraduate students!) but many elite colleges have also entered the game.

Stanford celebrity professors Sebastian Thrun and Peter Norvig made higher education history in 2011 when they offered their "Artificial Intelligence" class for free to anyone with an Internet connection. They were astounded when more than 160,000 people registered for the class, ushering in a new era for virtual education.

That course was successful mainly because of the high-quality professors and the Stanford name. But it also proved that this medium worked as a means to allow the best professors and the newest ideas to reach more people. Students benefitted from being able to watch lectures at convenient times, pausing or going back when needed. All the resources of the class, including homework and assessments, were available online, many of them built into the online course and giving immediate feedback.

Although many people dropped the Stanford "AI" class,

23,000 people finished, completing all the homework and passing the tests and exams. The top 1,000 finishers were contacted by the course professors, who assisted them in finding jobs in technology. Two hundred and fifty people received perfect scores, and none of them was a regular Stanford student.

Interestingly, the Stanford students who were registered for the live, campus-based Artificial Intelligence class ended up scoring a full letter-grade higher on the midterm and final exams than students in past years had scored. It turned out that most of the Stanford students skipped many of the live classes, opting instead for the online version. Something about this hybrid course, delivered online with occasional in-person classes, helped them to do better than their predecessors, who only had the option of the live class at a set time each week.

Sebastian Thrun went on to become the founder of Udacity, an affordable, interactive online course provider focused on technology. Courses at Udacity are referred to as Massive Open Online Courses (MOOCs) and are available to anyone. The two other big providers of MOOCs are Coursera and edX. MOOCs offer traditional course materials, such as videos, readings, and problem sets, but also provide interactive user forums that help build a community for students, professors, and teaching assistants. Elite universities such as Yale, Harvard, and Duke have also opened up many of their classes free of charge to the general public and have started offering thousands of lectures on their websites.

When courses in this medium were considered anything but rigorous or insightful, it wasn't known what would happen if great professors and institutions offered instruction in it. The last few years have shown that there is demand for high-quality online classes. We also now know that an online course is not an inferior product, and that some students actually perform better on this platform. There are many benefits of online courses, including flexible times, self-paced semesters, rewatching or pausing lectures, and built-in quizzes and feedback. Many courses use data analytics to measure a student's progress, enabling professors to make changes to the course while it is being taught. Some online classes won't allow a student to move forward to the next concept until she has mastered the previous one and proved it through online assessments.

Critics interject that online courses have no soul, no discussion, and no passion. They imagine a live college class to be full of debate and interested students, while they picture online courses as mechanical, with no learning from others and no going above and beyond the course material. These critics may be surprised to learn that students do engage, react, and discuss the course online, just as young people so easily connect on Twitter, Facebook, and other media.

The hybrid class, using both online and in-person sessions, may very well be the ideal. The "flipped classroom," in which students watch the lectures for homework and spend their live class time doing problems or in discussion with the professor, has been popular in recent years. Some experts believe that this sort of hybrid will be the way of the future: students will get the benefit of other schools' top professors and great online lectures, along with small group discussions on their home campuses.

Does this make you wonder why students would bother taking an Introduction to Economics class in a large lecture hall on their home campus when they could be part of an online class given by one of the best professors in the field? For now, the reason is that they can't always get credit for the online class. The credit and credential process is the second part of the online revolution, and it will be coming in due time.

The future is likely to bring exciting opportunities to students worldwide. Will they be able to take classes from top professors in their field, no matter which campus they call home? Will they form online study groups with students throughout the world? Will they get credit for courses based on their knowledge and progress rather than on the fact that they spent a semester in the course and met its basic requirements? Will it be possible to complete a class in less than a semester's time, or stretch it out longer without being penalized? We are on the frontier of a changing higher-education landscape that offers unlimited potential for the future.

THE UNBUNDLING OF THE COLLEGE EXPERIENCE

You used to have to buy a whole album in order to get your favorite song, but now you can download or buy songs individually. You used to subscribe to a cable channel to watch a premium show, but now you can buy only the episodes you want from Netflix. This is called "unbundling," or separating the charges for products or services that used to be sold as a package. This breaking up of charges is expected to come to higher education, bringing new cost savings and efficiencies.

Residential colleges usually charge by the semester, a lump sum that includes five classes, residence-hall fees, a meal-plan charge, activity fees, lab fees, and health-insurance fees. The cost is quoted by the year, with private universities charging up to $62,000 and many state schools asking for over $30,000 for in-state tuition. Financial aid is helpful, but it still leaves many families writing large checks and taking out sizable loans. Some colleges will enroll part-time students taking only a few courses, but the mainstream four-year residential colleges require students to pay for an entire semester's course load and fees. It is likely that this will become more flexible in the future.

There is one group of higher-education consumers that

has successfully unbundled the college experience. Adults over age twenty-five make up 38 percent of college students, and their priorities are convenience and low price.[120] Adult learners care very little about the extras of college life. They are often working adults who are juggling their coursework along with other duties, including supporting a family. Online colleges have become immensely popular among this group, offering a flexible and cost-effective way to get a degree.

Western Governors University (WGU) is the most cost-effective college option: it offers a full-time course load for only $6,000 a year, and some four-year bachelor's degrees for less than $25,000. It offers a high-quality program, yet it isn't as well-known as its rival the University of Phoenix. WGU is a fully accredited university founded by nineteen governors of western states, with the mission of expanding access to college education. The degree is fully online, with no frills, and is unbundled in the sense that students pay per course, without fees for residential life, computer labs, activities, or anything else not directly related to their particular courses. As the lone not-for-profit online university, WGU offers a bargain-priced degree that is starting to get nationwide attention.

Another low-cost means of working toward a degree is StraighterLine, which provides courses for as low as $49 after the student pays a $99 monthly fee. Students can complete a full year of coursework for under $1,500. StraighterLine does not offer a degree, but students can easily transfer credits to one of seventy partner colleges. The credits are also accepted by many member colleges of the American Council on Education (ACE) Credit College and University Network. The acceptance of credits by ACE is important because it suggests that any ACE colleges may accept a StraighterLine credit if asked to do so. Thus far, StraighterLine credits have been accepted for students earning degrees at many selective colleges, including Babson, Johns Hopkins, the University of Texas at Austin, and Cal State University.

One elite university has taken the unprecedented step of offering a bargain-priced online degree: Georgia Tech offers an online Master of Science in computer science in partnership with Udacity and AT&T. The online master's program maintains Georgia Tech's high standards, at a fraction of the cost of the on-campus program. Students accepted to the program will earn their Master of Science degree for only $7,000.

It is expected that many major universities will follow Georgia Tech's groundbreaking example. President Barack Obama lauded the program as a model for controlling the rising costs of higher education. Georgia Tech President G.P. "Bud" Peterson said, "As one of the leading technological universities in the United States, Georgia Tech is committed to helping students maximize the value of their educational investment."[121]

The popularity and success of the low-cost online college degree offers evidence that we are chipping away at the old model of a university. Does it make sense that an adult learner can get a bachelor's degree in business for $24,000 online, while a young adult on a private residential campus must pay ten times that much for the same degree?

Of course, the young adult is benefitting from the residential life experience: the clubs, career advice, computer labs, in-person classes, small group discussions with teaching assistants, and so much more. But considering the problems on college campuses today, is he really getting ten times more value than if he had completed an online degree?

Skeptics will be quick to respond that the graduate of an online university does not have the same career options as a graduate with a traditional degree. While that might be true *now*, we may look differently at the value of a degree in the future, especially if additional colleges of Georgia Tech's caliber start offering low-cost bachelor's degrees online.

THE FACULTY SUPERSTAR

Why are there more than two thousand psychology professors teaching Introduction to Psychology classes at colleges throughout the United States? In most cases, they lecture to hundreds of students on their campus, presenting the material to them at set times each week. There is usually little to no student-professor interaction in these large lecture classes, so watching the professor at the front of the room is no better than watching the professor on video from your dorm room. This moves us to the question of professor quality and whether a student would learn more from a better professor on a virtual network than from a lower-level professor on a local campus.

What makes one professor better than another? A good professor has a broad skill set, including expertise in her field, as well as the ability to craft her message to students and deliver it in an engaging way. Some professors excel in the delivery, others in the content, but those who are able to do both are superstars in the academic world. In the coming years, students are going to be increasingly drawn to these professors, which is likely to change the way they chose their classes.

"Would you rather watch Kenneth Branagh do Henry the Fifth, or see it at a community theater?" Professor Karl Ulrich from the Wharton School at the University of Pennsylvania asked *The New York Times*. "There are going to be some instructors who become more valuable in this new world because they master the new medium."

It is doubtful that the traditional four-year residential experience will ever go away. It will very likely continue as a premium experience for those who are willing to pay for it. But an "unbundling" of the college experience would offer students a less expensive way to earn a college degree.

Many good universities are oversubscribed, with limited space in dorms and classes. They could enroll more students by having them spend two or three years on campus, rather than four, and finish their degrees from home with online classes. That way, the university would have a full residential campus year-round, as well as a cohort of students working from home. The colleges could still offer a premium, four-year residential experience to those who want to pay for it.

No one knows exactly what the unbundling of college will look like, but you can guess that it will involve students transferring in lower-cost credits from other colleges, accelerating their degrees, spending less time in residence at college, and participating in online or hybrid classes on their own campuses. Virginia Tech already offers self-paced online math courses to freshmen, and these classes have had better results at lower costs.[122] Colleges may be opposed, since they will lose tuition dollars if they allow their courses to be replaced with cheaper alternatives, but there may be new revenue models that will allow the colleges to continue to prosper while the students save money.

THE COLLEGE EXIT EXAM

College students who thought they were finished with national exams after the SAT will be disappointed to know that college exit exams are on the horizon. Hiring managers have found that a college degree and GPA are not especially helpful to them in evaluating applicants to identify those who are ready for the workforce.

As we saw in Chapter Eight, 75 percent of employers want colleges to place more emphasis on critical thinking, complex problem-solving, written and oral communication, and applied knowledge in real-world settings. Employers are showing that they would welcome some means of measuring a graduate's abilities in these areas. Private organizations such as General Mills, Procter & Gamble, and Teach for America use their own in-house tests for job applicants and consider it an important part of the application process.

Several companies have developed and marketed assessment tests to serve this need, such as the ACT National Career Readiness Certificate and the ETS Proficiency Profile. But the test that has had the most traction is the Collegiate Learning Assessment, often referred to as the CLA+. In Chapter Three, we discussed the CLA, which is used by colleges to see how much their students improved in several measures between their freshman and senior years. The creators of the CLA recently adapted the test for individual use, so that a student can take the test independently and receive a score to show to potential employers. The ninety-minute test is scored on a 1,600-point scale, similar to the SAT, but that is where the similarities end. CLA+ is not multiple-choice; it is an open-ended test measuring critical thinking, analytical reasoning, document literacy, writing, and communication, and it costs only $35.

The CLA+ is offered to seniors at more than two hundred colleges, including the University of Texas and State University of New York systems. For students, it is a way to exhibit their skills and show their potential, and for employers, it is one way of screening for college graduates who are indeed ready for the workforce. Technically, it is not a true "exit exam," since it is unrelated to a student's degree status or grades. Like the SAT, it is a supplemental piece of information that students can choose to take to enhance their candidacy with employers.

Will such tests become widely considered by employers? If so, it will be a game-changer: during their college years, students will have to study harder, choose classes with more writing and critical-thinking assignments, and place a greater focus on academics. Students will be less likely to be judged on the admissions selectivity of their colleges, with more attention on how well they did on the CLA+ compared to other college students worldwide. For students at less selective or online colleges, this represents an opportunity to compete with and show better results than students at top-tier colleges. And for students who are attending elite colleges, a new focus on the CLA+ will mean that they must continue to progress academically during college and can no longer expect that employers will move their resume to the top of the pile based on their colleges' prestige.

DIGITAL BADGES: A NEW CREDENTIAL

The degree has been everything in higher education, the true reason students and parents are committing their time and money. The degree is supposed to show that a person has mastered her coursework and progressed in her field of study. Colleges have been trusted to award this credential only to those who have earned it, but employers are finding that many graduates are not ready for the workplace, and this has caused them to question the value of a college degree as the ultimate credential.

What if there were other ways of evaluating a student's skills and prospects? In the future, there may be an emphasis on "badges" or other certifications of a graduate's skills. Digital badges are credentials that represent skills, interests, and achievements earned through projects, programs, courses, or other activities. For example, the best accountants have a CPA, financial analysts can earn a CFA certification, and many fields require a license of some kind. We are already familiar with this type of credential and how it can enhance a resume.

New technology offers the possibility of moving this credential forward, so that we could see a widespread use of badges in multiple areas in the future. The John D. and Catherine T. MacArthur Foundation funded an initiative to expand the use of digital badges in a variety of professions. Digital badges are housed and managed online. It is hoped that employers will review a candidate's badges in order to validate their skills, so that they won't have to rely on the college degree alone.[123]

The Smithsonian's Cooper-Hewitt National Design Museum sponsors a badge for New York City high school students. Badges are awarded for achievement in design disciplines and overall design thinking. Students can earn badges at different intervals, and the highest-level badges are accredited by professional organizations such as the Council of Fashion Design in America (CFDA) and AIGA, the professional association for design. The earned badge is stored online, and students can display it to potential colleges or employers, demonstrating their design skill.

The sustainable agriculture program at UC Davis offers a badge system built on core competencies (distinctive and valuable skills) rather than course requirements or grades. The curriculum in the program is varied and hands-on, with lots of experiential learning that occurs outside the classroom, such as in fieldwork and internships. It is hard to capture that work and skill development in the confines of a regular class, so UC Davis chose to use a badge system to recognize skill development in several areas. One of the core competencies of the badge program is "systems-thinking" (the integration of societal, environmental, and economic perspectives into the analysis of a complex system). Students who earn this badge will have a link to their portfolios, in which employers can see the coursework and evidence of specific skills.[124]

Elite colleges are taking note of the interest in badges and professional credentials for students. Harvard Business School has launched an online learning initiative called HBX, and it is hoped that it will bring quality business education to a greater number of students. HBX offers a new program called Credentials of Readiness, or CORe, which is open to undergraduates, graduate students, and young adults who are typically not enrolled at Harvard. CORe is HBX's "primer on the fundamentals of business thinking," and it is designed to introduce students to the language of business. Students who are accepted to the program pay $1,500 (or less, with financial aid) to take three online courses (accounting, economics, and analytics) over a nine-week period. Not all students will pass the course, but those who do will be given a credential, noting a High Honors, Honors, or Pass finish to their course. CORe is brand-new (2014 was its inaugural year), but it is a unique opportunity. What liberal-arts graduate who hopes to get a job in business wouldn't want to take it?

Digital badges are in their infancy, and we don't know for sure whether they will gain credibility among employers, but they do seem to be on the rise. U.S. Department of Education Secretary Arne Duncan is a supporter who calls badges a "game-changing strategy."

Imagine two students applying for a job. One has a degree from Dartmouth with a high GPA, and his resume shows involvement in clubs and part-time jobs. The other job applicant graduated from Purdue and has several digital badges, in addition to work experience and club leadership. Employers look at his badges online and can see a portfolio of his work and achievements. They can see his competencies in addition to his grades, which gives them insight into the level of work he is likely to produce on the job. Which graduate would the firm hire? If his work was strong, it's likely they would hire the candidate with digital badges who was able to exhibit his abilities thoroughly.

TECHNOLOGY IN COLLEGE COURSEWORK

It's amazing to consider what technology will bring to the classroom in the future. We are already seeing adaptive learning and data analytics making their way into college and K–12 classrooms. We have also seen Khan Academy, an online "school" with a global reach, offer free and insightful lectures to students of all ages.

Adaptive learning uses computers to adjust the learning experience based on a student's progress. Questions and coursework become more difficult if learners are progressing well, and slow down if they need further instruction. My daughter's first-grade class uses Dreambox, which allows each child to complete math problems at his or her own level and pace. The program offers millions of paths through the system and goes beyond right and wrong answers, offering hints or strategies when needed.

Another option, popular at colleges today, is Learning Catalytics. It offers a "bring your own device" classroom intelligence system in which students use a computer or handheld device to participate in the lectures. The professor asks questions or gives students a problem to solve, and she is instantly given the results of how her students fared. The professor can see each individual's work, or look at results from the class as a whole. The system even indicates where responders are sitting in the classroom, so the instructor can see where the wrong answers are coming from. This real-time data gives a professor insight into how the class is doing and allows her to adjust her lecture if needed, or match up students in small group discussions based on their answers and need for help. With Learning Catalytics, the days of hiding in the back of the classroom are long gone!

A technology called Knewton allows the teacher to know every student's odds of passing a quiz before he even gives it. The teacher can see what concepts a student knows, and how deeply he understands them. When a student gets an incorrect answer on a test, the system can tell whether it was because of forgetfulness, lack of proficiency, a distraction, or something else altogether. In short, the technology knows more about the student than you would ever think is possible. Knewton's system infrastructure unlocks data that students have always produced, then uses it in the classroom to help the student succeed. My favorite application of the Knewton system is to tell a student what she should study tonight in order to be successful this week at school. It's amazing technology that will only grow in influence in the future and help students and teachers to work more efficiently and successfully in the classroom.

Finally, Khan Academy deserves some serious consideration. It is the largest "school" in the world, with more than ten million monthly users. This innovative non-profit with the goal of offering a "free world-class education for anyone anywhere" has brought education and hope to people in parts of the world without much of either. Khan Academy's worldwide reach is astounding, with lessons translated into more than thirty languages. It has come a long way from its founding, when Sal Khan posted short math lessons on YouTube while tutoring his young cousin. Those videos went viral and caught the attention of the world. Today there are thousands of lessons online.

Khan Academy is funded by donations from individuals and groups, such as Google and the Bill & Melinda Gates Foundation. Bill Gates is a fan of Khan Academy who actually uses it himself and with his children. He has called it "the future of education" and had this to say about its founder and prospects: "I see Sal Khan as a pioneer in an overall movement to use technology to let more and more people learn things and know where they stand. It is the start of a revolution."

The Khan Academy website (www.khanacademy.org) offers short instructional videos on various academic topics, with questions and solutions for the user to complete. I frequently recommend Khan Academy to the students I work with, since it offers a great way to review or build skills in math or science. A high school junior recently asked me to recommend a chemistry tutor to help her get a better grade in her class, but instead I advised her to spend an hour or two each week on Khan Academy's high school chemistry section. She started to understand chemistry at a deeper level, and her grade improved. Her parents were happy to see the good results without the cost of a private tutor, and they ended up dropping her Algebra II tutor and asking her to use Khan Academy in that area, too. She saw similar improvement in algebra, and she liked the ability to do the lessons at her convenience.

You can learn almost anything on Khan Academy. It offers excellent SAT review sessions and was recently tapped by the College Board to design free, world-class test prep for the "new" SAT, which goes live in 2016. Besides classes in math, science, astronomy, history, philosophy, and many other subject areas, Khan Academy presents lessons prepared by experts at its partner organizations, including the Museum of Modern Art, the J. Paul Getty Museum, the Stanford School of Medicine, and NASA.

The Khan Academy platform is easy to use, with intuitive, straightforward lessons. Questions at the end of each lesson assure that the student has comprehended the material. My own elementary-school-aged children love the Khan

Academy lessons for their age group, and it is fun for them to realize that children from all over the world are using the same examples that they are.

HIGHER EDUCATION IN THE FUTURE

We are on a path to a "big bang" change in higher education. No one knows exactly what college will look like in ten years or in twenty years, but it's safe to say that it will look drastically different than it does today. The whole education sector, from kindergarten through grad school, is on the cusp of massive and lasting change that I believe will be of great benefit to all types of learners. We are likely to see more online learning, accelerated degrees, assessments and badges for graduates, and technology impacting the classroom in new and exciting ways. There will be less focus on "getting in" to college, and more focus on building skills and achievements while there. The "brand name" of a college may be less meaningful, since graduates will be judged on so many more important measures than the admissions selectivity of their colleges.

Online education has been called the "Great Disruption" in higher education, since it is expected to shake up the status quo. Some people feel that online education and the unbundling of the college experience will lead to great cost savings and benefits to the student. Others feel that online education is a poor substitute for traditional classroom-based learning, and that it will not improve outcomes or experiences.

There are more than 2,700 four-year colleges in the United States today, and it is not likely that they will all survive these changes. Some colleges are already facing competition to enroll students, which is essential to fund the colleges' operating expenses. Colleges have taken on a lot of debt to build and maintain campus amenities. Without a steady number of students, they will face major challenges.

A REIMAGINED UNIVERSITY: MINERVA

Would you like to spend your college years living in several of the great cities of the world, studying in a hybrid program that includes MOOCs from top professors and small, discussion-heavy seminars on your own campus?

Minerva is a new, "reimagined" university that opened in the fall of 2014. Students live in "global residence halls," starting in San Francisco their first year and changing locations every semester after that. Students will become immersed in the cultures of Buenos Aires, Berlin, Hong Kong, Sydney, Cape Town, and other cities. They won't have access to intercollegiate sports, campus dining halls, and college libraries, but they will benefit from a rigorous academic program and the chance to become a citizen of the world.

Minerva is a for-profit venture founded by Ben Nelson, former CEO of Snapfish. He is joined on the board by Larry Summers, former US Secretary of the Treasury and Harvard president, and Bob Kerrey, former US senator and president of the New School. Nelson hopes to shake up the elite-college monopoly and offer a modern rival to colleges such as Stanford and Harvard. One thing he has on his side is the cost. Tuition is less than half the price of most private colleges in the United States. The first cohort of Minerva students were ready to embark on their journey in the fall of 2014, and it will be interesting to see if this new entrant to the college market changes the playing field for elite colleges.

There are experts who predict that a thousand colleges will close, while others estimate that it will be only a few hundred. While we don't know the future, it is important for students entering college now to be aware of the changes that could occur in higher education during their lifetimes. Taking out extensive loans today to attend a college that may be bankrupt and held in lower esteem in fifteen years is not a good decision.

Online education is here to stay, and it will rock the higher education world over the next ten years. Students should think beyond the traditional model and look at developing their skills in order to be successful in the changing world.

Myths and Misunderstandings about College and Admissions

"What are the top colleges looking for, anyway?"
When I meet with parents of high school–aged students, this is the number-one thing they want to talk about. Just when they got used to the idea that college admissions is all about the SAT score, suddenly more and more colleges aren't even requiring it. They become sure that having a special talent is the key, yet their soccer-playing daughter is denied admission and one of her classmates not involved in extracurricular activities is admitted.

"What more could my son have possibly done?" one father asked as he rattled off his son's achievements, all impressive, after getting an early-admission deferral from an Ivy League college.

"It's all a mystery," another mother said as she described how a student at her daughter's school ranked fifteenth in her high school class was admitted to Stanford over several higher-ranked students.

It is not the goal of this book to help parents figure out how to get their child into an elite college. However, to get into any college, it is important to understand the admissions process, and breaking through some popular myths about college life can also yield insight that can help students build their Success Profiles.

ADMISSIONS MYTHS

Colleges like well-rounded students, and everyone should play at least one sport.

Colleges like a well-rounded *class*, full of kids who are different from one another and excel at different things. If a student is a superstar in one area (for example, a concert violinist, a published author, or a student who spearheaded a major community-service project), most colleges—even elite ones—would not expect him to also excel at a sport. Students should explore what interests them, and should try to build some expertise and accomplishment in one or two areas. They can focus on areas where they have a passion or can make an impact, either locally or nationally. It's not necessary to add superfluous activities just for the sake of an admissions committee that won't be too impressed anyway.

"Legacy" students with a parent who attended a particular school will automatically get accepted there.

If only it were that easy! Many colleges could fill their entire freshman class with alumni children, some twice over. While it is true that the acceptance rate for alumni children is higher, their average SAT scores and grade point averages are usually only slightly lower than those of the incoming class as a whole. So yes, alumni children do get a boost, but it will not typically propel a B student to an Ivy League college. For example, at Yale, three out of four alumni children are denied admission, despite their favored status.[125] It's also interesting to note a few of the colleges that give no alumni preference whatsoever: Caltech, MIT, the

University of California at Berkeley, Texas A&M, and the Universities of Cambridge and Oxford in England.

If your parent donates a lot of money to a college, you are sure to get in.

Colleges will look carefully at an applicant whose parents are nationally known in their field or able to make large donations. This type of applicant is sometimes called a "development case," referring to the development (or fundraising) office of the college. But if you are hoping to impress Harvard, keep in mind that its endowment is worth $32 billion, so your family would have to donate quite a lot of money to get the committee's attention. There are more than seventy US college and university systems with endowments greater than $1 billion. Donations of several thousand dollars, or even twenty thousand dollars, are not even a blip on their radar screens.

A client told me that he had donated $5,000 each year to Dartmouth, his alma mater, in hopes of showing a high level of alumni engagement that would increase the chances of acceptance for his son. He did this at the expense of 529 college savings plan contributions and thus needed to take out parent and student loans for college. He was especially upset when his son was denied admission at Dartmouth. We will never know for sure what goes on in admissions-committee evaluations regarding alumni children and contributions, but it's likely that a regular $200 donation is valued just as much as a $5,000 or even $10,000 contribution.

The *Stanford Magazine* (a publication of the Stanford Alumni Association) ran an article by Ivan Maisel that discussed the admissions process in detail. Maisel indicated that Debra von Bargen, the assistant dean of admissions, is the point person for dealing with alumni. "When an applicant indicates that he or she is a legacy, the admissions office checks with the Alumni Association, which responds not only with a yes or no but also an indication of whether the alum in question has maintained his or her connection to the school," he wrote.

"Sometimes people say, 'Do you know I've given money? Do you know I've led (this committee)?'" von Bargen says. "We really don't. We know which people are engaged. But exactly what they do, *how much they give, we have no idea*" (italics added for emphasis).[126]

If a very influential person, like the President of the United States, writes a recommendation letter for you, you are sure to get accepted.

If the child of a world leader applies to college, it is likely that he or she will indeed have a lot of options. College-admissions deans will be eager to enroll this student because of the worldwide recognition they would get from having a child of such a leader choose their school. There is also the potential that this world leader would speak on campus, offer connections, or make a large donation. But if this same world leader recommended the child of a friend or colleague for admission, none of this would happen. When influential people recommend applicants who are not their own children, colleges do not see positive press, speaking engagements, or contributions. In that sense, it is not very compelling to the admissions committee, particularly if the leader does not know the student personally and is only writing the letter as a courtesy.

I was at a college admissions conference when an Ivy League admissions dean was asked about what he thinks of letters from United States presidents. He admitted that they are fun to get and are saved for their historical value, but he went on to say that they don't have an impact on the admissions status of the student.

If you get a perfect 2400 SAT score, you will most likely get into
any school where you apply.

This statement is false, as the odds are still against you.
For example, over the last five years, sixty-nine percent of
Stanford applicants with a perfect SAT score were denied.
Only 10 percent of applicants with a perfect 800 math score
were admitted, and 14 percent of those with a perfect verbal
score were accepted.

Elite colleges prefer students from private high schools. They
have relationships with prep-school guidance counselors that
ensure that their students get in. Public school students are at a
disadvantage.

The majority of students at elite colleges graduated from
public high schools. For example, 61 percent of Princeton
freshmen are from public high schools, and 70 percent of
Harvard students came from public schools. Of course, most
students in the total population (90 percent) attend public
school, so it is logical that we find a greater percentage of
them at top colleges.

The real question that most parents have is whether attending an elite private school, such as Exeter or Andover,
will give their student a boost in admission prospects. Do the
private school "name brand" or counselor connections offer
any boost? My opinion is that they do not. College admissions officers are traveling the world, turning over every rock
looking for bright students and ensuring that the doors to
their colleges are open to all types of kids. They talk frequently to guidance counselors from both public and private
schools. They deny many qualified students from elite prep
schools each year.

While I don't believe that the private school name or connections will offer any advantage in the admissions process,
I do believe that the private school experience may position
the student to be more successful in both high school and

college. Many independent schools have extensive reading and writing assignments, and some have roundtable discussion classes and a focus on critical-thinking skills. These practices have been proven to benefit the student in the long run. Some private schools offer learning-support services and are able to help kids succeed who weren't able to thrive in a large public-school environment. It's important to note that not all private schools offer these types of programs, and indeed, many public schools are exceptionally strong in these areas. Every family should evaluate their local options carefully.

Colleges' stated graduation rate is not an important measure, since I know I will be graduating regardless of whether the other students graduate on time.

Every student should look carefully at the freshman retention rate and graduation rate of all colleges that they are considering, because it is an important measure of academic quality. Popular and well-funded colleges have freshmen retention rates of 90 percent of more, meaning that fewer than 10 percent of the freshmen drop out or transfer. Some elite colleges, such as Yale and Dartmouth, have a 99-percent freshmen retention rate, and selective state universities such as UCLA, Michigan, and Virginia retain more than 96 percent of their freshmen.

Colleges that only retain 65 or 70 percent of their freshmen should be looked at with caution. If you do decide to attend a college with a low graduation rate or freshmen retention rate, you should be especially diligent in creating a plan for support and success before you start classes.

Homeschoolers don't have a strong enough academic background to get into a top college, or to excel at college once they get there.

Homeschooled students are found at every elite college in the country. College admission offices get a large enough number of applications from homeschoolers that they now post guidelines for them on their websites. The admissions officers take the time to review each student's entire curriculum, as well as their achievements and testing in full. Those who think of homeschoolers as students focused on specific religious values may be surprised to find that many families choose to homeschool their children out of a desire to promote their intellectual and creative development, and that many homeschooled students are doing interesting and advanced work. Princeton's valedictorian in 2004 was homeschooled until college, and I have personally worked with homeschooled students whose intellectual achievements were amazing.

One of the points of this book is that all students should forge their own paths and develop the expertise that they will need to be successful in life. There are homeschoolers who have taken this belief to heart at a young age, and who have developed their own curriculum that includes extensive reading, writing, and critical thinking. Alongside their independent studies at home, they also often take advantage of opportunities described in Chapter 6; homeschooled students who are accepted at top colleges have usually taken community college courses or online college courses, or were enrolled in the Stanford online high school.

Hiring an independent educational consultant is a waste of time and money.

For full disclosure, I am an independent educational consultant (IEC) and am a big proponent of an IEC's role in college admissions. I believe that ethically responsible IECs are an invaluable part of the college admissions landscape. They offer families advice about finding good-fit colleges, exploring options, and navigating the admissions and testing processes. Many are knowledgeable about financial fit and financial aid, and they are skilled at working with families and encouraging the student to stay at the center of the process.

Some people feel that high school guidance counselors should do this for free. However, a typical guidance counselor has extensive in-school duties, including helping students build their schedules, organizing in-school standardized testing, and working through personal problems with students on an individual level. Are they also expected to visit more than thirty colleges a year, as many IECs do? Should they be staying up to date on unusual majors, the sports recruiting process, and how to find value in the college process? The reality is that the college admissions environment has become multifaceted, and there is room for IECs to add value.

This is probably a relief to high school guidance counselors, since on average they have a caseload of 471 students. In California, a typical guidance counselor works with more than one thousand students. There is obviously demand for IECs, and a Lipman Hearne study in 2013 found that 26 percent of "high achieving" seniors (those scoring above the mean on the SAT and ACT), used an IEC in the college search or application process.

Families considering hiring an IEC should be sure that the consultant is a member of the Independent Educational Consultants Association (IECA). This is the gold standard for IECs; membership requires credentials and adherence to an ethical code. IECA has more than 1,300 member consultants, and you can find a great one near you in the organization's online directory at www.iecaonline.org. If you are concerned about cost, keep in mind that nearly all IECA member consultants work pro bono or at a reduced rate with several students each year. Low-income families who need help with the admissions process can also consider programs such as Questbridge, SEO Scholars, Let's Get Ready, or Upward Bound.

My neighbor's son got a scholarship to Princeton. They are wealthy and it had nothing to do with financial need.

Princeton and other Ivy League colleges reserve all their grant money for students with financial need. They do not offer any merit scholarships or grants to students for reasons other than financial need.

I saw a graduation program that listed a student as winning the "Rotary Scholarship to Cornell University" and I can see where that might make people think that the student won a full $60,000 merit scholarship to Cornell. But it was actually a $500 scholarship given by his local Rotary Club, which would have been good at whatever college he attended. Sometimes students do earn merit scholarships from outside sources, but the majority of elite colleges reserve their own grant money for students with need.

I'll never get into a top college because I am bad at math.

First, anyone who feels that he is "bad at math" should take that sentiment out of his mind, since it is rarely true. Maybe you don't do well at math because you don't spend enough time working through the problems, or you've mentally decided that you are bad at it and the results follow. A good attitude about math and lots of practice are likely to improve your results.

Elite colleges are looking for students who are very strong academically and have other special talents. For example, an accomplished writer who has math grades that are good, but not outstanding, may still get accepted to top colleges. But if you are finishing high school and your grades and test scores are truly deficient, then yes, you are unlikely to get into an elite college. Once you get to college, resist the temptation to blow off math; take a class that challenges you and keep practicing. Regardless of your eventual career choice, the thinking skills that math develops will help you.

*Colleges have an equal number of male and female students,
and they admit both genders in equal ratios.*

For most of their history, top colleges were a bastion for
men, so it is surprising that some selective schools are now
faced with significantly more applications from women.
Overall, women make up 57 percent of undergraduate students and 60 percent of degree earners.

In order to keep the gender ratio in balance, certain liberal-
arts colleges and universities offer men an admissions advantage, normally because they lack engineering or business
programs, which are especially attractive to men. Examples of
selective colleges that have many more applications from females than males include University of North Carolina at
Chapel Hill, College of William & Mary, Tulane University,
New York University, and Middlebury College. Conversely, at
MIT, women are given the advantage: just over 5,400 females
applied recently (alongside more than 12,000 males), yielding
a class that was 46 percent female, proof that women had a
higher acceptance rate. At the Ivy League schools, there is a
roughly equal number of male and female applicants, so the
gender imbalance does not come into play.

*It's not necessary to visit colleges until after you get accepted
and see what your choices are.*

The college visit is an important way for students and
their parents to get a feel for the campus and hear about its
programs directly from a student. It is not advisable to wait
until after decisions are released, since that is leaving the
important evaluation process until the very end.

Visiting a college is an important way for the admissions
committee to evaluate a student's level of interest in their
school. But if costs or time restraints keep you from making
a trip, be sure to meet with an admissions officer visiting
your high school or to talk with a representative at a college

fair or information reception. With the numbers of applications increasing each year, a show of "demonstrated interest" is an important part of the admissions process.

COLLEGE LIFE MYTHS

College tuition is the one investment that always pays off, since no one can take away your education and it stays with you your whole life.

While it is true that a college degree is yours for life, unfortunately, the same can sometimes be said for student loans. Debt from mortgages, credit cards, or car loans can be discharged in bankruptcy, but student-loan debt is the only type that stays with you until death, unless it is paid off.

The question about whether a specific college's tuition is a good investment is one that each student must evaluate and consider for himself. We cannot assume that all investments in college will pay off financially in the long run. It is important for students to consider college to be the first big investment of their lives and to weigh the different options in pricing and financing.

The quality of the academic program is better at private colleges than at state colleges.

There are more than 2,700 four-year colleges in the United States, and their quality is not determined by whether they are privately run or state-funded. There are many top-quality public universities, and conversely, there are some private colleges with low graduation rates and low standards. When evaluating colleges, keep in mind that there are small, selective honors colleges within large state universities, as well as public liberal-arts colleges, where you can experience a unique community and educational program. Plus, of course, you can get a "top college" experience anywhere by developing your Success Profile.

Employers and recruiters do not look as favorably on state college graduates.

A recent study by the *Wall Street Journal* showed that employers recruit most heavily at state universities and are happy with the employees that they find there.[127] Penn State, the University of Illinois, and Purdue each host more than four hundred recruiting companies every year, which is double the number at many private colleges. These universities, along with Texas A&M, were named the favorite colleges among companies hiring entry-level workers in the *WSJ* report. This study was interesting because of its size and breadth; reporters interviewed hiring managers at corporations, non-profits, and government agencies, who were collectively responsible for hiring more than forty-three thousand college seniors from more than 130 schools.

Employers preferred to interview at large state universities for several reasons: they felt that these graduates are academically prepared, have had the most relevant training for their company, and are likely to stay at their firms for many years. There are also economies of scale at play, in that the employers can reach many students with one campus visit and with one corporate-college relationship. In contrast, more than half of Harvard graduates will go to graduate school, either immediately after graduation or within a few years, so recruiters won't meet as many students who are interested in working at their firms for the long term.

Of course, for firms hiring only a small number of employees, a visit to a smaller campus is effective enough. There are several investment banks and consulting firms that favor elite colleges, both private and public, but don't recruit at the universities named in the *WSJ* survey.

Getting into college is the hard part; once I'm there I can finally relax.

This myth is prevalent among students today, and it leads to a missed opportunity for growth and advancement during college. The job market for young adults is very tough, so it's surprising that so many young adults see college as a vacation rather than a time to prepare for their futures. At college, students can develop a new perspective, meet students from all over the world, make new friends, and grow in independence, but let's not forget that it is also time to improve skills in critical thinking, writing, and complex problem-solving and get ready for a career.

Students who get into Ivy League schools are so smart that they don't have to study as much as other college students.

Students at Ivy League and other top-performing colleges tend to study more than the national average. The Arum and Roksa study described in *Academically Adrift* showed that elite-college students spent more time on the most-important solitary study time, averaging three hours more studying-alone time per week than their peers at other colleges.[128]

Majoring in subjects such as English and theater is a bad idea, since you will never get a job that way.

Plenty of career paths begin with English, theater, and other liberal-arts majors. If writing is what you truly enjoy and excel in, you can major in English and pursue a job at a magazine, publishing house, tutoring company, or other area that prizes English degrees. If acting or designing sets is your dream, you may be able to parlay your theater degree into a job at a local playhouse, a theater production company, or a non-profit that teaches musical theater to children. These are just a few examples, and I could name many more.

If you are worried about the lower income that may

accompany some of these jobs, keep in mind that there are always exceptions to the rule that graduates with certain majors earn more than others. English and theater graduates often have strong communication and critical thinking skills, which are important to employers. Aidan and Julie, two of my former clients, did very well for themselves when they studied subjects that interested them.

Aidan is a graduate of the prestigious drama program at the Tisch School at NYU. His rigorous conservatory training, strong verbal ability, and intense work ethic made him an appealing candidate to many employers. He took several business and economics courses while at NYU, and he was able to land a job at a hedge fund.

Julie was an English major at Northwestern who loved writing and analyzing literature. She wanted a high-paying career with a clear path for advancement that would let her work with other smart professionals. She chose a career in consulting and was hired by Accenture.

Joining clubs or activities at college is nice, but it has no real value in the long run.

Students who are involved in college life report greater satisfaction with college, stronger grades, more improvement in critical-thinking and complex problem-solving skills, and increased likelihood of career success and well-being in the future. Almost any activity that pulls a student into college life, such as a sport, a club, or even a fraternity or sorority, has a positive influence.

Success in college does not require a plan—just show up.

Ambitious young people go to college with a plan. They know what they hope to accomplish, and they decide how often and when they will study. They think about what it takes to stick to their plan. Some students go to college with a goal but have no idea about how to go about achieving it, and they can be sidetracked by minor disappointments or diversions.

What are top colleges looking for, anyway?

Many elite colleges deny more than 90 percent of students who apply. If, after all we've covered, you are still wondering what the special formula for acceptance is, you should know that it isn't really such a mystery.

Colleges openly display their accepted-student profiles, and you can see that the admitted students at top US colleges have testing in the top fifth percentile worldwide, along with high grades. You can also see that they usually accept students from all fifty states and many countries, making more difficult odds for students in some regions and better chances for those in others. Colleges also look for students with a global worldview, compassion, grit, and the ability to be innovative and forward-thinking. Finally, they are looking for students who have achieved something extraordinary. A national ranking in tennis, a Siemens science-fair prize, a chess championship trophy, or a beautiful art portfolio all give evidence of a student's bright future.

While it is true that it is difficult to get admitted to an elite college, one of the biggest myths is that this even matters. The ultimate myth is that young people should spend their high school years focused on test prep, crafting themselves into ideal applicants, and then taking on whatever loans necessary to cover an elite college education. The idea of "getting into college" has replaced true learning and achievement. A student is better off taking charge of her own education and future, and developing the skills and attitudes she needs to be successful, rather than focusing on getting a college to accept her. In reality, it's the student, not the college, that determines future success and happiness.

Success Profile Worksheets

ACT I

1. Develop a growth mindset (page 66).

Select one:

Do you believe that it is mainly your talent and abilities that
lead to your success?
YES / NO

Do you believe that your intelligence is fixed and there isn't
anything you can do to change it?
YES / NO

If you answered "yes" to these questions, you may have a fixed
mindset, which can be limiting.

Suggested Action: Read Carol Dweck's book, *Mindset: The
New Psychology of Success.*

2. Start on a path toward a sense of purpose (page 68).

What issue(s) in the world are you worried about or would
you like to help with?

_____

_____

Is there a local issue that concerns you? Brainstorm ways to
get involved with it.

_____

_____

Which industries or career interests would you like to learn more about?

_____

_____

How can you learn more about these issues or fields? Who can you meet with to discuss them or learn about them firsthand?

_____

_____

List at least one person you know who you can help in some small or large way.

_____

_____

3. Explore areas of academic interest in depth (page 73).

List three academic areas that you would like to learn more about, then add three ways you can explore each interest.

1. _____
2. _____
3. _____

What is your goal for your academic exploration, and how will you measure your progress?

_____

_____

4. Devise and execute a plan to improve your academic performance (page 74).

Review the suggested study strategies on pages 75-78. Which one(s) do you think would work best for you, and why?

_____

_____

Create a study plan for the coming week, then check off each item as you complete it. (See page 78)

5. Improve your writing, critical thinking, and complex problem-solving skills (page 78).

Define what each skill means to you and list times when you expect to use them in your life.

Critical thinking:

_____

_____

Complex problem-solving:

_____

_____

Writing:

_____

_____

List three things you can do to improve in these areas.

1. _____
2. _____
3. _____

6. Make an impact in an area of interest (page 81).

Consider your community and school, and review your answers to step 2 and 3. What is one area in which you can make a positive impact?

_____

_____

What is the impact you can make? Set a goal and draft a plan for how you will reach it. Give yourself concrete steps and deadlines.

_____

_____

DATE:		
SUBJECT: _____		
SUBJECT: _____		
SUBJECT: _____		
SUBJECT: _____		
SUBJECT: _____		

ACT II

1. Do not take on more than a reasonable amount of student-loan debt (page 99).

Determine your EFC with an online calculator. Discuss a budget for college expenses with your family.

Consider what your life will be like after college graduation, and calculate how much debt you are comfortable having.

How much do you expect to make per year?

Anticipated annual salary: _____

Divide that by 12 to find your monthly income, then make a rough estimate of your after-tax income by multiplying your projected monthly income by .75.

Anticipated after-tax monthly income:

_____

Calculate your anticipated costs of living per month (include rent, utilities, transportation, groceries, other shopping, entertainment, savings, et cetera).

Approximate monthly costs: _____

Subtract your monthly costs from your anticipated after-tax monthly income.

Amount left over for loan payments and other needs:

_____

Make sure that this amount is *at least* enough for the minimum monthly payment on any loans you intend to take out.

2. Have a goal and a plan for college (page 100).

What do you hope to accomplish in college?

_____

_____

List three areas in which you plan to improve during college.

1. _____
2. _____
3. _____

Write down your academic goals for this semester, and read them every day.

_____

_____

3. Get an "Ivy League" education at whatever college you attend (page 102).

List three ways in which you can take advantage of your college's resources.

1. _____
2. _____
3. _____

List three professors you would like to build a relationship with and at least one way in which you plan to do it.

1. _____
2. _____
3. _____

Write down your criteria for choosing your next semester's courses.

_____

_____

Look over your list. Are your criteria in a reasonable priority order? If not, reorganize them.

_____

_____

4. Develop skills and routines that help you adapt and excel in college (page 109).

What are a few things you can do to ensure that you are physically and emotionally well during your time at college?

_____

_____

Write a schedule for a typical week in college, including time for classes, studying, work, and play. (See page 111)

Suggested Action: Join a new activity or group at college.

5. Focus on paid employment and internships (page 112).

What are three things that you can do in the next six months to increase your chances of getting an internship?

1. _____

2. _____

3. _____

Suggested Actions: Write your resume, join LinkedIn, visit your campus career center.

6. Develop communication skills, both spoken and written (page 115).

What are three ways in which you can improve your professional presentation?

1. _____

2. _____

3. _____

Suggested Action: Write at least one item a day, even if it is only a properly punctuated email.

7. Work in a team. If possible, lead a team (page 116).

List your plans for teamwork during your college career. What teams or groups do you plan to be involved with, and is there leadership opportunity?

_____

_____

8. Step out of your comfort zone (page 117).

Connect with at least three people from a different background than your own. What did you learn from them?

_____

_____

DATE:	MONDAY	TUESDAY
TIME: _____		
TIME: _____		
TIME: _____		
TIME: _____		
TIME: _____		

WEDNESDAY	THURSDAY	FRIDAY	SATURDAT	SUNDAY

Directory of Awards, Honors, and Fascinating Experiences for High School Students

ARTS AWARDS

American Alliance for Theater Education Student Video Award
http://www.aate.com/?page=videocontest
Congressional Art Competition
http://www.house.gov/content/educate/art_competition/
Gutenberg Award for Graphic Arts
http://www.igaea.org/International-Graphic-Arts-Education-Association/gutenberg-award.html
National Young Arts Competition
http://www.youngarts.org/
Physics Photography Contest
http://www.aapt.org/programs/contests/photocontest.cfm
Scholastic Art & Writing Awards
www.artandwriting.org
Smithsonian National Portrait Gallery Teen Portrait Contest
http://www.npgteenportrait.org/
Student Editorial Cartoon Contest
http://www.knowledgeunlimited.com/cartoon/cartofweek.html
US Presidential Scholars in the Arts
www.youngarts.org

CITIZENSHIP AWARDS:

Boy Scout Eagle Award
http://scoutingnewsroom.org/about-the-bsa/fact-sheets/eagle-scouts/
DAR Good Citizens Award
http://www.dar.org/national-society/education/youth-programs
Girl Scout Gold Award
https://www.girlscouts.org/mygoldaward/default.aspx
Peace First Prize
www.peacefirst.org

COMPUTER SCIENCE

Google Code In Awards

http://www.google-melange.com/gci/homepage/google/gci2012
MIT Think Awards
http://think.mit.edu/

ENGINEERING AWARDS

Air Force Association Cyber Patriot Competition
www.uscyberpatriot.org
Best Robotics Award
http://best.eng.auburn.edu/b_general_rules.php
Engineering Encounters Bridge Building Contest
www.bridgecontest.org
First Robotics Challenge
www.usfirst.org/roboticsprograms
NASCAR Stem Initiative: Student Racing Challenge
www.studentracingchallenge.com
NASA Space Settlement Design Contest
http://settlement.arc.nasa.gov/Contest/
NASA Human Exploration Rover Challenge
http://www.nasa.gov/roverchallenge/home/
National Robotics Challenge
http://www.nationalroboticschallenge.org/joomla/
TEAMS: Engineering Tests
http://teams.tsaweb.org/

ENVIRONMENTAL AWARDS

AMNH Young Naturalist Awards
http://www.amnh.org/learn-teach/young-naturalist-awards
Brower Youth Awards
http://www.broweryouthawards.org/
Envirothon
www.envirothon.org
Living on the Ocean Planet Video Contest
http://nosb.org/competitions-2/nosb-video-contest/
President's Environmental Youth Awards
http://www2.epa.gov/education/
    presidents-environmental-youth-award
Siemens We Can Change the World Challenge
http://www.wecanchange.com/

GOVERNMENT AWARDS

Boys State/Boys Nation
http://www.legion.org/boysnation
The Congressional Award
www.congressionalaward.org

Girls State/Girls Nation
https://www.alaforveterans.org/Programs/
    ALA-Girls-State-Locations/
United States Senate Youth Program
http://www.ussenateyouth.org/

INTERNATIONAL YOUTH AWARDS

Duke of Edinburgh International Youth Award
www.dofeusa.org
Rotary Youth Leadership Award
https://www.rotary.org/en/rotaract-interact-and-ryla
Summit Youth Award
http://www.youthaward.org/

LANGUAGE AWARDS

National Classics Exam
www.aclclassics.org
National French Exam
www.frenchteachers.org/concours
National German Exam
www.aatg.org
National Latin Exam
www.nle.org
National Security Language Initiative Scholarship Award
http://www.nsliforyouth.org/
National Spanish Exam
www.nationalspanishexam.org

MATH AWARDS

American Mathematics Competitions
http://www.maa.org/math-competitions
American Regions Math League Competitions
www.arml.com
Harvard-MIT Math Tournament
http://web.mit.edu/hmmt/www/
High School Fed Challenge
http://www.federalreserveeducation.org/resources/classroom/
    competitions/fed-challenge/
Moody's Mega Math Challenge
http://m3challenge.siam.org/
National Economics Challenge
http://www.councilforeconed.org/events/
    national-economics-challenge/

USAMTS Math Contest
http://www.usamts.org/

MISCELLANEOUS or MULTIPLE SUBJECT AWARDS

Davidson Fellows
http://www.davidsongifted.org/fellows/
National History Day Contest
http://www.nhd.org/Contest.htm
National Geological Society Rubincam Youth Award
http://www.ngsgenealogy.org/cs/rubincam_youth_award/
    nomination_form
Rachel Carson Sense of Wonder Competition
http://www.epa.gov/aging/carson/index.htm
Spirit of Innovation Awards
http://www.conradawards.org/
US Presidential Scholars Program
http://www2.ed.gov/programs/psp/index.html

MUSIC AWARDS

BMI Student Composer Awards
http://www.bmifoundation.org/program/
    bmi_student_composer_awards
Glenn Miller Birthplace Society Music Scholarship Award
http://www.glennmiller.org/scholarships.html
MTNA Instrumental Competitions
http://www.mtna.org/programs/competitions/performance-
    competitions-guidelines/
NFMC Instrumental Competitions
http://www.nfmc-music.org/index.
    php?src=gendocs&ref=Competition%20%26%20Awards
US Presidential Scholars in the Arts
www.youngarts.org

SCIENCE AWARDS

BioGENEius Challenge
http://www.biotechinstitute.org/go.cfm?do=page.view&pid=2
Discovery Channel Young Scientist Challenge
http://www.youngscientistchallenge.com/
DuPont Challenge Science Essay Contest
http://thechallenge.dupont.com/
Edison Innovation Induction Award
http://www.edisonawards.com/

Google Science Fair
https://www.googlesciencefair.com/en/
Intel Science & Engineering Fair Awards
http://www.intel.com/content/www/us/en/education/competitions/
    international-science-and-engineering-fair.html
Intel Science Talent Search
http://www.intel.com/content/www/us/en/education/competitions/
    science-talent-search.html
MIT Inspire
www.inspirehumanities.mit.edu
National Young Astronomer Award
http://www.astroleague.org/al/awards/nyaa/noya.html
Physics Photography Contest
http://www.aapt.org/programs/contests/photocontest.cfm
Siemens Competition in Math & Science
http://www.siemens-foundation.org/en/siemens_competition_
    archive.htm
Spirit of Innovation Awards
http://www.conradawards.org/
Stockholm Junior Water Prize
http://www.siwi.org/prizes/stockholmjuniorwaterprize/
Toshiba Exploravision Awards
http://www.exploravision.org/

SPEECH & DEBATE AWARDS

American Legion Oratorical Contest
http://www.legion.org/oratorical
National Forensics League Tournament
www.nationalforensicsleague.org
NMA Leadership Speech Contest
http://www.nma1.org/Speech_Contest/Speech_Contest.html
Optimist International Oratorical Award
http://www.optimist.org/e/member/scholarships4.cfm
Poetry Out Loud: National Recitation Contest
http://www.poetryoutloud.org/competition/national-finals
Sons of American Revolution Oratorical Contest
http://www.sar.org/Youth/Oration_Contest_Procedures
Voice of Democracy Award
http://www.vfw.org/Community/Voice-of-Democracy/

SPORTS AWARDS

Presidential Physical Fitness Award
https://www.presidentschallenge.org/

Wendy's High School Heisman
http://www.wendyshighschoolheisman.com/

VOLUNTEER AWARDS

Barron Prize for Young Heroes
www.barronprize.org
Build a Bear Huggable Hero Award
http://heroes.buildabear.com/HuggableHeroes.aspx
Do Something Award
https://www.dosomething.org/awards
Kohl's Cares Youth Awards
http://www.kohlscorporation.com/CommunityRelations/
    scholarship/
Jefferson Awards for Public Service
http://www.jeffersonawards.org/programs
Presidential Volunteer Service Awards
http://www.presidentialserviceawards.gov/
Prudential Spirit of Community Award
http://spirit.prudential.com/view/page/soc

WRITING AWARDS: POETRY

JHU Creative Minds Poetry Award
http://cty.jhu.edu/imagine/guidelines/contest/creativeminds.html
Kenyon Review Poetry Prize for Young Writers
http://www.kenyonreview.org/contests/patricia-grodd/
NFSP Poetry Awards
http://www.nfsps.com/poetry_contests.htm
Princeton Secondary School Poetry Prize
http://www.princeton.edu/arts/lewis_center/high-school-contests/
Smith College Poetry Prize for Girls
http://www.smith.edu/poetrycenter/highschoolprize/

WRITING AWARDS: CREATIVE WRITING

Bennington College Young Writers Competition
http://www.bennington.edu/youngwritersawards.aspx
Claremont Review Awards
http://www.theclaremontreview.ca/html/annualcontestsubmissions.
    html
JHU Creative Minds Fiction Award
http://cty.jhu.edu/imagine/guidelines/contest/creativeminds.html
National Young Playwrights Competition
http://www.youngplaywrights.org/national-competition/
Scholastic Art & Writing Awards

http://www.artandwriting.org/
US Presidential Scholars in the Arts Award
http://www.youngarts.org/us-presidential-scholars-arts

WRITING AWARDS: ESSAYS

American Foreign Service Association High School Essay Contest
http://www.afsa.org/essay_contest.aspx
The Atlantic & College Board Writing Prize
https://www.collegeboard.org/writing-prize?affiliateId=cbhomehero
    &bannerId=writingprize-Slot1
Ayn Rand Essay Contest
http://aynrandnovels.org/essay-contests.html
Bill of Rights Institute "Being an American" Writing Contest
http://billofrightsinstitute.org/programs-events/students-programs-
    events/contest/
Claremont Review Writing Contest
www.theclaremontreview.ca/contest
Civil War Essay Contest
http://www.gilderlehrman.org/programs-exhibitions/civil-war-
    essay-contest
Colonial Dames of America Essay Contest for Washington
    Workshops Congressional Seminar
https://www.nscda.org/site3/ps/pa_ww.php
Daughters of the American Revolution Essay Contests
http://www.dar.org/natsociety/essays.cfm
Diverse Minds Writing Challenge
http://www.bnaibrith.org/diverse-minds.html
Dupont Challenge Science Essay Contest
http://thechallenge.dupont.com/
FRA Americanism Essay Contest
http://www.fra.org/Content/fra/AboutFRA/EssayContest/default.cfm
The Fire Free Speech Award
http://www.thefire.org/student-network/essay-contest/
Holocaust Remembrance Essay Contest
http://www.holocaustresources.org/2015-herc-essay-contest-2/
Jane Austen Society
http://www.jasna.org/essaycontest/
Letters for Literature Contest
http://www.read.gov/letters/
Listen to a Life Contest
http://www.legacyproject.org/contests/ltal.html
National Council of Teachers of English/Norman Mailer Award
http://www.ncte.org/awards/student/nmwa

National History Day Writing Contest
http://www.nhd.org/CategoryPaper.htm
Optimist International Essay Contest
http://www.optimist.org/e/member/scholarships3.cfm
Penguin Signet Classics Student Scholarship Essay Contest
http://www.us.penguingroup.com/pages/services-academic/essay-
home.html
Profile in Courage Award Essay Contest
http://www.jfklibrary.org/Education/Profile-in-Courage-Essay-
Contest.aspx
Ralph Waldo Emerson Prize/Concord Review
http://www.tcr.org/tcr/emerson.htm
Society of Professional Journalists High School Essay
https://www.spj.org/a-hs.asp
Sons of the American Revolution Knight Essay
http://www.sar.org/Youth/Knight_Essay_Contacts
Tribute to Rescuers Essay Contest
http://archive.adl.org/tribute_to_rescuers/essays.asp
US Institute of Peace, National Peace Essay Contest
http://www.usip.org/category/course-type/
national-peace-essay-contest
Voice of Democracy Award
http://www.vfw.org/Community/Voice-of-Democracy/
World Wide Waldens Live Deliberately Essay Contest
http://www.worldwidewaldens.org/essay-contest/
The Writers Conference, Inc. Writing Contest
http://www.writingconference.com/contest.htm

FREE SUMMER PROGRAMS

Clark Scholars Program
http://www.depts.ttu.edu/honors/clark_scholars/
Governor's School
Twenty-three of the fifty US states offer tuition-free summer programs for high school residents. Check with your high school for
nomination procedures.
Internship in Biomedical Research at NIH
https://www.training.nih.gov/programs/sip
MIT Research Science Institute (RSI)
http://www.cee.org/research-science-institute
Research & Engineering Apprenticeship Program (REAP)
http://www.aas-world.org/REAP/REAPprogram.html
Rockefeller University Summer Outreach
http://www.rockefeller.edu/outreach/highschoolapp

Ross Mathematics Program (charge for room and board only)
https://people.math.osu.edu/ross//
Sharpe Art Foundation Summer Seminar
http://sharpeartfdn.qwestoffice.net/summer1.htm
Stanford Institute of Medicine Summer Program for High School
    Juniors
http://simr.stanford.edu/
Telluride Association Summer Program
http://www.tellurideassociation.org/programs/high_school_
    students/tasp/tasp_general_info.html
Women's Technology Program at MIT
http://wtp.mit.edu/

Notes

1   Alison Leigh Cowan, "Remembering When College Was a Buyer's Bazaar," The Choice, *New York Times* website, March 31, 2011, http://thechoice.blogs.nytimes.com/2011/03/31/remembering-when-college-was-a-buyers-bazaar

2   Jerome Karabel, *The Chosen: The Hidden History of Admissions and Exclusion at Harvard, Yale, and Princeton* (New York: Houghton Mifflin Harcourt, 2005), 44.

3   Ibid., 123.

4   Ibid., 124.

5   Ibid., 125.

6   Ibid., 125.

7   Ibid., 127.

8   Ibid., 127.

9   Ibid., 183.

10 Ibid., 188.

11 Ibid., 267.

12 Ibid., 269.

13 Ibid., 270.

14 Ibid., 379, 389–99.

15 Cornell Trustees, "Cornell Undergraduate Tuition, Fees, Room and Board: 1990–91 through 2009–10" (trustee minutes; Financial Plan/ Operating and Capital, Cornell University, June 2009). http://dpb.cornell.edu/documents/1000212.pdf

16 Drew Desilver, "Record number of international students studying in U.S." (Pew Research Center, *FactTank: News in the Numbers*, November 12, 2013). *http://www.pewresearch.org/fact-tank/2013/11/12/record-number-of-international-students-studying-in-u-s/*

17 Kevin Eagan, Jennifer B. Lozano, Sylvia Hurtado, and Matthew H. Case, *The American Freshman: National Norms Fall 2013* (Los Angeles: Higher Education Research Institute, UCLA, 2013). http://www.heri.ucla.edu/monographs/TheAmericanFreshman2013.pdf

18 Andrew Murr, "A Little Extra Help," *Newsweek*, July 31, 2004. http://www.newsweek.com/little-extra-help-130335

19 United States Securities and Exchange Commission, *Annual Report Pursuant To Section 13 Or 15(D) Of The Securities Exchange Act Of 1934 For The Fiscal Year Ended December 31, 2012, Commission file number 1-6714,*

The Washington Post Company, Form 10-K (Washington, DC). http://www.sec.gov/Archives/edgar/data/104889/000010488913000009/d10k.htm

20 Nick Anderson, "Five colleges misreported data to U.S. News, raising concerns about rankings, reputation," *Washington Post* (February 6, 2013). http://www.washingtonpost.com/local/education/five-colleges-misreported-data-to-us-news-raising-concerns-about-rankings-reputation/2013/02/06/cb437876-6b17-11e2-af53-7b2b2a7510a8_story.html

21 Ry Rivard, "Micro-Targeting Students," *Inside Higher Ed* (October 24, 2013). http://www.insidehighered.com/news/2013/10/24/political-campaign-style-targeting-comes-student-search

22 "5 Things You Need to Know About College Admission," BigFuture by the College Board, 2014, https://bigfuture.collegeboard.org/get-in/applying-101/5-things-you-need-to-know-about-college-admission

23 Gallup, Inc., "Great Jobs Great Lives: The 2014 Gallup-Purdue Index Report" (Washington, DC: Gallup, Inc., 2014), 3.

24 Ibid., 4.

25 Ibid., 7.

26 Phil Izzo, "Congratulations to Class of 2014, Most Indebted Ever," *Wall Street Journal* (May 16, 2014). http://blogs.wsj.com/numbers/congratulations-to-class-of-2014-the-most-indebted-ever-1368/

27 Stacy Berg Dale and Alan B. Krueger, "Estimating the Payoff to Attending a More Selective College: An Application of Selection on Observables and Unobservables," NBER Working Paper No. 7322 (August 1999). http://www.nber.org/papers/w7322

28 Stacy Berg Dale and Alan B. Krueger, "Estimating the Return to College Selectivity over the Career Using Administrative Earnings Data," NBER Working Paper No. 17159 (June 2011). http://www.nber.org/papers/w17159

29 Princeton University, "Elite Colleges Not Necessarily Best Ticket to High Earnings," news release, July 16, 2008, https://www.princeton.edu/pr/news/00/q1/0126-krueger.htm

30 David Leonhardt, "Revisiting the Value of Elite Colleges," Economix, *New York Times* website (February 21, 2011). http://economix.blogs.nytimes.com/2011/02/21/revisiting-the-value-of-elite-colleges/?_php=true&_type=blogs&_r=0

31 Ibid.

32 Valerie J. Calderon and Preety Sidhu, "Business Leaders Say Knowledge Trumps College Pedigree," Gallup, Inc. website, February 25, 2014. http://www.gallup.com/poll/167546/business-leaders-say-knowledge-trumps-college-pedigree.aspx

33 Stacy Berg Dale and Alan B. Krueger, "Estimating the Return to College Selectivity over the Career Using Administrative Earnings Data," NBER Working Paper No. 17159 (June 2011). http://www.nber.org/papers/w17159

34 Gladwell, Malcolm, *David and Goliath: Underdogs, Misfits, and the Art of Battling Giants* (New York: Little, Brown, 2013).

35 Ibid., 83.

36   Ibid., 85.
37   Jillian Anthony, "World's Top Employers for New Grads," *CNN*,
     September 25, 2014. http://money.cnn.com/gallery/pf/
     jobs/2014/09/23/top-employers-for-new-grads/
38   Stan Phelps, "Cracking Into Google: 15 Reasons Why More Than 2
     Million People Apply Each Year," *Forbes*, August 5, 2014. http://www.
     forbes.com/sites/stanphelps/2014/08/05/cracking-into-google-the-
     15-reasons-why-over-2-million-people-apply-each-year/
39   Thomas L. Friedman, "How to Get a Job at Google, Part 2," *New York
     Times*, April 19, 2014. http://www.nytimes.com/2014/04/20/opinion/
     sunday/friedman-how-to-get-a-job-at-google-part-2.html
40   Thomas L. Friedman, "How to Get a Job at Google," *New York Times*,
     February 22, 2014. http://www.nytimes.com/2014/02/23/opinion/
     sunday/friedman-how-to-get-a-job-at-google.html
41   Ibid.
42   Thomas L. Friedman, "How to Get a Job at Google, Part 2," *New York
     Times*, April 19, 2014. http://www.nytimes.com/2014/04/20/opinion/
     sunday/friedman-how-to-get-a-job-at-google-part-2.html
43   Peter Osterlund, "Parisa Tabriz, Google's 'security princess,'
     talks about college," *60 Second Recap*, October 10, 2013. http://
     www.60secondrecap.com/parisa-tabriz-google-security-princess/
44   Clare Malone, "The Hacker," *Elle*, July 8, 2014. http://www.elle.com/
     life-love/society-career/google-parisa-tabriz-profile-2
45   Kim Parker, Amanda Lenhart, and Kathleen Moore, "The Digital Revo-
     lution and Higher Education," *Pew Research Internet Project*, August 28,
     2011. http://www.pewinternet.org/2011/08/28/the-digital-revolution-
     and-higher-education/
46   Brad Plumer, "Only 27 percent of college grads have a job related to
     their major," *The Washington Post*, May 20, 2013. http://www.
     washingtonpost.com/blogs/wonkblog/wp/2013/05/20/only-27-percent-
     of-college-grads-have-a-job-related-to-their-major/
47   Courtney Rubin, "Making a Splash on Campus," *New York Times*, Sep-
     tember 19, 2014. http://www.nytimes.com/2014/09/21/fashion/college-
     recreation-now-includes-pool-parties-and-river-rides.html?_r=0
48   Richard Arum and Josipa Roksa, *Academically Adrift: Limited Learning
     on College Campuses* (Chicago: The University of Chicago Press, 2011),
     4.
49   Catherine Rampell, "A History of College Grade Inflation," *Economix*,
     July 14, 2011. http://economix.blogs.nytimes.com/2011/07/14/the-
     history-of-college-grade-inflation/
50   *Academically Adrift*, 1.
51   Richard Arum and Josipa Roksa, *Aspiring Adults Adrift* (Chicago: The
     University of Chicago Press, 2014), 133.
52   Ann Saphir, "Skip college, forfeit $800,000: Fed study," *Reuters*, May 5,
     2014. http://www.reuters.com/article/2014/05/05/us-usa-fed-college-
     idUSBREA440KD20140505
53   United States Department of Labor, Board of Labor Statistics, "Usual
     Weekly Earnings Summary," news release, October 24, 2014, http://

www.bls.gov/news.release/wkyeng.nr0.htm

54   United States Department of Labor, Board of Labor Statistics, "Labor Force Statistics from the Current Population Survey," news release, October 3, 2014, http://www.bls.gov/web/empsit/cpseea05.htm

55   "The Rising Cost of Not Going to College," Pew Research Social & Demographic Trends (February 11, 2014). http://www.pewsocialtrends.org/2014/02/11/the-rising-cost-of-not-going-to-college/

56   The Thiel Foundation, "About the Fellowship." Accessed September 19, 2014. http://www.thielfellowship.org/about/about-the-fellowship/

57   Carol S. Dweck, *Mindset: The New Psychology of Success* (New York: Ballantine Books, 2006), 41.

58   Ibid., 23.

59   Ibid., 23.

60   Ibid., 23.

61   Ibid., 61.

62   William Damon, *The Path to Purpose: Helping our Children Find Their Calling in Life* (New York: Free Press, 2008), 14–15.

63   Ibid., 33.

64   Ibid., 23.

65   Angela Lee Duckworth, "Personal Grit as Key to Success," *PBS*, May 7, 2013. http://www.pbs.org/wnet/ted-talks-education/speaker/dr-angela-lee-duckworth/

66   Deborah Perkins-Gough, "The Significance of Grit: A Conversation with Angela Lee Duckworth," *ASCD*, September 2013. http://www.ascd.org/publications/educational-leadership/sept13/vol71/num01/The-Significance-of-Grit@-A-Conversation-with-Angela-Lee-Duckworth.aspx

67   Ibid.

68   Beth J. Harpaz, "Princeton Review to Stop Claiming 255-Point Boost In Test Scores," *The Huffington Post* (May 17, 2010). http://www.huffingtonpost.com/2010/05/17/princeton-review-to-stop-_n_579363.html

69   Melissa Korn, "Bosses Seek 'Critical Thinking,' but What Is That?" *Wall Street Journal* (October 21, 2014). http://online.wsj.com/articles/bosses-seek-critical-thinking-but-what-is-that-1413923730

70   Joe Lau and Jonathan Chan, "[Tutorial C01] What is critical thinking?" Opencourseware on Critical Thinking, Logic, and Creativity, accessed November 4, 2014. http://philosophy.hku.hk/think/critical/ct.php

71   Eddy Ramirez, "More High School Kids Take College Classes," *US News*, June 26, 2008. http://www.usnews.com/education/articles/2008/06/26/more-high-school-kids-take-college-classes

72   Meta Brown, Sydnee Caldwell, and Sarah Sutherland, "Just Released: Young Student Borrowers on the Sidelines of the Housing Market in 2013," *Liberty Street Economics*, May 13, 2014. http://libertystreeteconomics.newyorkfed.org/2014/05/just-released-young-student-loan-borrowers-remained-on-the-sidelines-of-the-housing-market-in-2013.html#.VDIHm2d0w7Z

73   Andrew Roberts, *The Thinking Student's Guide to College: 75 Tips for Getting a Better Education* (Chicago: University of Chicago Press, 2010), 53.

74   Ibid.

75   Ibid.

76   Lynn O'Shaughnessy, "New study shows careers and college majors often don't match," *CBS News*, November 15, 2013. http://www.cbsnews.com/news/new-study-shows-careers-and-college-majors-often-dont-match/

77   Arum and Roksa, 69.

78   Ibid., 100.

79   Gallup, Inc., "Great Jobs Great Lives: The 2014 Gallup-Purdue Index Report" (Washington, DC: Gallup, Inc., 2014), 3.

80   Julie Ray and Stephanie Kafka, "Life in College Matters for Life After College," *Gallup,* May 6, 2014. http://www.gallup.com/poll/168848/life-college-matters-life-college.aspx

81   Valerie Strauss, "Why college freshmen need to take Emotions 101," *The Washington Post,* September 28, 2014. http://www.washingtonpost.com/blogs/answer-sheet/wp/2014/09/28/why-college-freshmen-need-to-take-emotions-101/

82   "How Does Your Student Feel? Four Keys to Emotional Intelligence," *College Parent Central,* June, 2011. http://www.collegeparentcentral.com/2011/06/how-does-your-student-feel-four-keys-to-emotional-intelligence/

83   Claudia Allen, "Choosing Target Colleges and Universities—Research from NACE," DirectEmployers (April 15, 2014). http://www.directemployers.org/2014/04/15/choosing-target-colleges-and-universities-research-from-nace/

84   Emily Fredrix, "Students Paying Internship Search Firms," *The Washington Post* (March 6, 2007). http://www.washingtonpost.com/wp-dyn/content/article/2007/03/06/AR2007030600544_pf.html

85   Hal M. Bundrick, "The One Thing College Grads Need that Makes Them 3 Times More Likely to Get Job Offers," MainStreet (June 4, 2014). http://business-news.thestreet.com/mainline-media-news/story/the-one-thing-college-grads-need-makes-them-3-times-more-likely-get-job-offers/1

86   Leah Hyslop, "'Surprising' amount of British students studying overseas," *Telegraph,* February 21, 2011. http://www.telegraph.co.uk/education/expateducation/8333579/Surprising-amount-of-British-students-studying-overseas.html

87   Institute of International Education, "Open Doors 2013: International Students in the United States and Study Abroad by American Students are at All-Time High," press release, November 11, 2013, http://www.iie.org/Who-We-Are/News-and-Events/Press-Center/Press-releases/2013/2013-11-11-Open-Doors-Data

88   Paul Bedard, "Harvard: Just 6 in 19 Millennials have jobs, half are part-time," *Washington Examiner,* February 7, 2013. http://washingtonexaminer.com/harvard-just-6-in-10-millennials-have-jobs-half-are-part-time/article/2520719

89   Richard Fry, A Rising Share of Young Adults Live in Their Parents' Homes," *Pew Research,* August 1, 2013. http://www.pewsocialtrends.org/2013/08/01/a-rising-share-of-young-adults-live-in-their-parents-home/

90   Deborah L. Jacobs, "How to Stop Playing Resume Roulette," *Forbes*, June 24, 2014. http://www.forbes.com/sites/deborahljacobs/2014/06/24/how-to-stop-playing-resume-roulette/

91   Victoria Taylor, "Engineering majors make the most money: study," *NY Daily News*, September 10, 2013. http://www.nydailynews.com/life style/top-10-highest-lowest-paying-college-majors-article-1.1451161

92   *It Takes More than a Major: Employer Priorities for College Learning and Student Success* (Washington, DC: Association of American Colleges and Universities and Hart Research Associates, 2013). https://www.aacu.org/leap/presidentstrust/compact/2013SurveySummary

93   Ibid.

94   "The Skills and Qualities Employers Value Most in Their New Hires," National Association of Colleges and Employers, press release, April 24, 2014. http://www.naceweb.org/about-us/press/skills-employers-value-in-new-hires.aspx

95   *How Should Colleges Prepare Students to Succeed in Today's Global Economy?* (Washington, DC: Peter D. Hart Research Associates, 2007). http://www.aacu.org/sites/default/files/files/LEAP/2007_full_report_leap.pdf

96   Dan Schwabel, "The Multi-Generational Job Search Study 2014," *Millennial Branding*, May 20, 2014. http://millennialbranding.com/2014/multi-generational-job-search-study-2014/

97   Cory Weinberg, "Morgan Stanley Rejected Almost 89,000 Summer Hires This Year," *Bloomberg Businessweek*, June 24, 2014. http://www.businessweek.com/articles/2014-06-24/around-90-000-interns-applied-to-morgan-stanley-this-summer

98   Hilary Stout, "The Coveted but Elusive Summer Internship," *The New York Times*, July 2, 2010. http://www.nytimes.com/2010/07/04/fashion/04Internship.html

99   Chandlee Bryan, "Insider Q & A: Chris Hoyt on How to Get a Job at Pepsi," *StartWire*, December 16, 2011. http://www.startwire.com/blog/14148112673-3

100   Dan Schwabel, "National Survey Finds College Doesn't Prepare Students for Job Search," Millennial Branding, May 20, 2014. http://millennialbranding.com/2014/multi-generational-job-search-study-2014/

101   Katy Wachtel, "A Guide to Getting Your Dream Job at Goldman Sachs," *Business Insider*, January 28, 2011. http://www.businessinsider.com/goldman-sachs-interview-job?op=1

102   Dan Patrick, "On becoming a SC anchor," *ESPN*, December 6, 2001. http://espn.go.com/talent/danpatrick/s/2001/0830/1245784.html

103   National Center for Education Statistics.

104   Bureau of Labor Statistics.

105   Susannah Snider, "3 Must-Know Facts About For-Profit Colleges, Student Debt," *U.S. News and World Report*, October 1, 2014. http://www.usnews.com/education/best-colleges/paying-for-college/articles/2014/10/01/3-facts-for-students-to-know-about-for-profit-colleges-and-student-debt

106   Ibid.

107   U.S. Department of Education, "Federal Student Aid," https://studentaid.ed.gov

108   Susannah Snider, "Colleges and Universities That Claim to Meet Full Financial Need," *US News*, September 15, 2014. http://www.usnews.com/education/best-colleges/paying-for-college/articles/2014/09/15/colleges-and-universities-that-claim-to-meet-full-financial-need

109   Homepage, MeritAid.com (beta), accessed November 4, 2014, http://www.meritaid.com

110   David Leonhart, "Top Colleges, Largely for the Elite," *New York Times*, May 24, 2011. http://www.nytimes.com/2011/05/25/business/economy/25leonhardt.html?pagewanted=all

111   David Leonhart, "'A National Admissions Office' for Low-Income Strivers," *New York Times*, September 16, 2014. http://www.nytimes.com/2014/09/16/upshot/a-national-admissions-office-for-low-income-strivers.html?abt=0002&abg=0

112   Edvisors, "Expert Insights on Planning and Paying for College." http://www.edvisors.com/

113   http://www.acct.org/pell-grants

114   Hadley Malcolm, "Millennials' ball-and-chain: Student loan debt." *USA Today*, July 1, 2013.

115   Gallup, Inc., "Great Jobs Great Lives: The 2014 Gallup-Purdue Index Report" (Washington, DC: Gallup, Inc., 2014), 3.

116   Halah Touryalai, "Student Loan Problems: One Third of Millennials Regret Going to College," *Forbes*, May 22, 2013. http://www.forbes.com/sites/halahtouryalai/2013/05/22/student-loan-problems-one-third-of-millennials-regret-going-to-college/

117   Jordan Weissmann, "Here's Exactly How Much the Government Would Have to Spend to Make Public College Tuition-Free," *The Atlantic*, January 3, 2014. http://www.theatlantic.com/business/archive/2014/01/heres-exactly-how-much-the-government-would-have-to-spend-to-make-public-college-tuition-free/282803/

118   PayScale, "2013 College Education ROI Rankings." http://www.payscale.com/college-education-value-2013

119   Ryan Lytle, "Study: Online Education Continues Growth," *US News*, November 11, 2011. http://www.usnews.com/education/online-education/articles/2011/11/11/study-online-education-continues-growth

120   Jovita M.M. Ross-Gordon, "Research on Adult Learners: Supporting the Needs of a Student Population That Is No Longer Nontraditional," *Association of American Colleges and Universities*. http://www.aacu.org/publications-research/periodicals/research-adult-learners-supporting-needs-student-population-no

121   "Obama Cites Georgia Tech's OMS CS as Future Model of College Affordability," *Georgia Tech*, August 22, 2013. http://www.cc.gatech.edu/news/obama-cites-georgia-tech%E2%80%99s-oms-cs-future-model-college-affordability

122   Tamar Lewin, "Master's Degree is New Frontier of Study Online," *New York Times*, August 17, 2013. http://www.nytimes.com/2013/08/18/education/masters-degree-is-new-frontier-of-study-online.html?pagewanted=all

123 "Project Q&A With: Design Exchange," *Hastac,* July 1, 2013. http://
     www.hastac.org/wiki/project-qa-design-exchange
124 Paul Fain, "Badging From Within," *Inside Higher Ed,* January 3, 2014.
     https://www.insidehighered.com/news/2014/01/03/uc-daviss-ground-
     breaking-digital-badge-system-new-sustainable-agriculture-program
125 Max Nisen, "Legacies Still Get A Staggeringly Unfair College Admis-
     sions Advantage," *Business Insider,* June 5, 2013. http://www.business
     insider.com/legacy-kids-have-an-admissions-advantage-2013-6
126 Ivan Maisel, "What It Takes," *Stanford Alumni,* November 2013. https://
     alumni.stanford.edu/get/page/magazine/article/?article_id=66225
127 Teri Evans, "Penn State Tops Recruiter Rankings," *Wall Street Journal,*
     September 13, 2010. http://online.wsj.com/articles/SB10001424052748
     7043589045754776433369663352
128 Richard Arum and Josipa Roksa, *Academically Adrift: Limited Learning on
     College Campuses* (Chicago: The University of Chicago Press, 2011), 4.

Acknowledgments

I could not have written *It's the Student, Not the College* without the contributions and encouragement of many colleagues, clients, and family members. I am so thankful for the people who helped me, as well as for those who shared the stories and experiences that were included in the book.

I owe a special thanks to my agent, Jacqueline Flynn from Joelle Delbourgo Associates, who believed in the project, offered valuable insight, and helped me to shape its message. I was lucky to find an agent who is patient, has a great sense of humor, and appreciates a contrarian view of the college admissions world.

It was a pleasure working with the team at The Experiment. I'd like to thank Molly Cavanaugh, who amazed me with her editing. She had great enthusiasm for the book and I was so happy to have her skilled editing and valuable insights and suggestions. I want to thank the publisher, Matthew Lore, for taking on *It's the Student, Not the College* as the first education book on The Experiment's list. I appreciate the tireless efforts of Stuart Calderwood, Jennifer Hergenroeder, and Karen Giangreco.

I have worked with so many families over the last twelve years in my consulting business and I think it is fair to say that I learned something from each of them. They shared their triumphs and struggles with me, and I thank them for letting me into their lives. I am especially grateful to the parents who allowed me to review their financial aid forms and decision results. The cases in chapter ten would not have been insightful without the openness of these families. The many studies, surveys, and other books mentioned throughout *It's the Student, Not the College* were crucial in bringing facts and data to the book, and I appreciate the work put into these projects, since they benefitted this book so very much.

A special thank you goes to my husband, Michael White, who was a true partner in the writing of this book. Whether it was research, finding charts and data for me, reading chapters, or offering ideas or encouragement, he was always there for me and I am so thankful for that. My daughters, Caroline, Julianne, and Evie will be happy to see their names in print twice in this book, and that is one small way of thanking them for giving up some mommy time this year.

Index

About the Author

KRISTIN WHITE is an educational consultant who helps students evaluate colleges and other educational opportunities, while also helping them navigate the admissions process. Kristin's educational consulting firm, Darien Academic Advisors, LLC, is based in Darien, Connecticut, but works with students from all over the United States and the world. In the last ten years, she has worked with families from nineteen different countries and twenty states. Kristin is a member of the New England Association for College Admissions Counseling and the Independent Educational Consultants Association, where she is a member of the Outreach Committee. She is a graduate of Georgetown University and has an MBA from the University of Texas–Austin.

Kristin is also the author of *The Complete Guide to the Gap Year: The Best Things to Do Between High School and College*, published by Jossey-Bass in 2009.